SECRETS

of

REVIVAL

Dr. R. Edward Miller

Copyright © 1995 by Dr. R. Edward Miller, Author

ISBN: 0-945818-10-6

All rights reserved. No part of this book may be reproduced or transmitted in any form or by any means, electronic or mechanical, including photocopying, recording or by any information storage and retrieval system, without permission in writing from the author.

Photo by: Marco N. Porcile

Illustrations by: Norbert Senftleben

Foreword

God has privileged me to witness first hand many major worldwide revivals, and God has revealed to me many of the principles that accompany the outpouring of grace from on High that constitutes a revival.

In the story of Gideon, many of those principles are acted out by Gideon and his men. I have not tried to uncover those principles, first, because we like formulas and progressive steps to success, and second, because God in His sovereignty does not follow formulas: nevertheless, His principles do remain intact. Rather, I have left them in story form that he that has eyes may see and that the hungry heart will find meat to eat.

Not only are the secrets of revival hidden throughout this historical event in the life of Israel, but God used this entire event in the history of Israel to foretell again – through prototype – the story of Jesus and Redemption. This event shows that through the Sacrifice of Jesus on the Cross and through faith in that Sacrifice, many souls would be delivered from all their enemies.

The story of Gideon is a history exceedingly rich in types and symbols. In symbolic details it depicts the work of Jesus overcoming the Satanic enemies of mankind. The pitcher and torch illustrate the Crucifixion. The trumpet sounds aloud the cry repeated by Martin Luther, *Justification by*

Faith. *"For by grace are ye saved through faith; and that not of yourselves: it is the gift of God" (Ephesians 2:8).*

The details of the entire story of the interaction of God and Gideon – the weapons used and the process of development of God's men – richly portray the ways and means to revival and the battle of deliverance from spiritual oppression.

Contents

1. Devastation 1
2. The Question 9
3. God Begins To Work 19
4. Message Of A Prophet 27
5. A Strange Visitor 37
6. Gideon's Searching Heart Finds
   An Answer 43
7. Gideon Looks Within 53
8. Not Impossible 63
9. Gideon Asks For Proof 73
10. His Eyes Were Opened 85
11. Jehovah Shalom 93
12. "Gideon, Clean Your Own Back Yard" 101
13. Revelation Awaits Obedience 109
14. Revival Needs A Man Of Faith And Valor 123
15. God With Gideon 131
16. 32,000 Said, "Let's Go" 141
17. Gideon's Faith Tried 149
18. Gideon's Army? 157
19. God Chooses His Men 165
20. Meat For Gideon's Men 175
21. Men On The Mountaintop 183
22. The Sword Of Gideon 193
23. Gideon Worshiped 199
24. Divided They Will Conquer 207

25.	The Battle Of The Trumpets	217
26.	Burning Torches — Wounded Wood?	223
27.	"Look On Me"	233
28.	"Attack, Attack, Attack!"	241
29.	Victory	251
30.	His Name Is Gideon	259

1

Devastation

An intense young Jew of the tribe of Manasseh strode angrily through the vandal-ravaged fields of his father's farm early that morning. His black bushy beard, that accented his angular features, visibly indicated his distress as it danced in cadence to his irate muttering. Tall, broad of shoulder and fearless in his anger, he thundered aloud to the mocking winds his defiant curses and vowed vengeance upon the pitiless Midianite marauders that had invaded and pillaged his grain fields that night.

"All these months of labor have been in vain," he growled to himself. "They have destroyed my crops and robbed us again of our food. What we will eat this coming winter, only God knows." As he thought of that Name, he cried out, "God? What God? Our old God, Jehovah, has abandoned us, and our worship of Baal also has proved useless. Baal has proved himself impotent to help us." As he walked, he raged in fear, frustration, and anger. Yet, he felt more defiant than ever.

It was a warm sunny day in midspring, already late in the year for resowing. The fields that yesterday were sprouting green with promise of a rich harvest, now looked as if some violent tempest had ravaged them. However, it was not the mindless powers of nature that had worked this distressing ruin before his eyes. That would have been an evil much easier to tolerate. But he well knew that the malicious, spiteful Midianites had seen his promising fields and in their vicious hatred had deliberately destroyed his fields.

Israel had lost the war with the Midianites, and ever since their defeat, their conquerors sought every opportunity to oppress and destroy them. In malevolent glee they had demolished their crops, spoiled their fields and stolen their cattle. Furthermore, they would kill anyone who complained or showed any animosity.

He had worked his fields cautiously and even surreptitiously — working only in the late evenings and as quietly as a mole. But in spite of his caution, the enemy had discovered his labors and ravaged his work. "Has some neighbor betrayed me and led them to my labors?" he wondered. He was aware that sometimes a destitute Israelite, breaking under the strain of his distress and degradation, would betray a courageous neighbor to the enemy for the pitiful bribe of an ephah of grain.

In burning fury the young man contemplated the ruin before his eyes. How graphically real it made the dire straits forced upon him. They were a conquered people; their enemies, the Midianites, lost no opportunity to make life as onerous as possible for them. They incessantly spied on the Israelites, and every promising grain field they found, they vengefully destroyed.

The animosity of the Midianites for the Jews knew no limits. They pitied no one! Old or young, widows or incapacitated, impoverished or sick — all were grist for their mill of bitter hatred. They exulted in devastation and eagerly sought the ruin of the defeated Hebrews at every opportunity. They had no remorse for their evil — not even a twinge of conscience troubled them. If those Jews whose fields they destroyed died of hunger, they laughed and jested at their untimely demise. It gave the enemy more pleasure to have them die a slow miserable death of starvation than to slay them outright with the sword.

The Israelites, who still outlived the terrible oppression, feared that if things continued like this much longer their whole nation would succumb. For seven interminable, intolerable years Israel had endured the devastating destruction. Despicable poverty and deadly starvation were the allotment the Midianites daily measured out to them. Since their defeat in battle, they had known nothing but fear and misery.

At times some desperate, determined soul took the risk and sowed some obscure portion of his field. But more often than not, before that sowing could be harvested, keen-eyed bands of spying Midianites would find and destroy it. Furthermore, if they found him at his labors, they would destroy him along with his field.

This young descendent of Manasseh, a son of Joseph, stared in bitter fury as he looked upon the latest destruction of the Midianites. Six weeks before this day he had dared to sow his early barley in spite of them, but they had come that night and utterly wiped out his flourishing green fields. It was fortunate that they had not caught him working there for they would have tortured and slain him for daring to attempt to provide sustenance for his family.

Audacious Defiance

As his enraged eyes gazed on the tragic devastation before him, a consuming challenge — fueled by his flaming anger — arose in his heart against their ruthless oppressors. Instead of yielding to cringing fear and abject discouragement, a reckless feeling of defiance possessed him.

Smashing his fist into his palm, he shouted resolutely to himself, "By the living God of Israel, if He still lives, I will defy them. I know of a valley quite hidden beyond yonder hills. No one lives there now, poor souls; they were slain in the battle. I will go there alone at night and sow those abandoned fields myself."

He smiled grimly to himself as he planned his strategy. "I will work only at night and tell absolutely no one — not even my own family! Very quietly I will slip away while the family is sleeping and sow and harvest those fields right under the enemy's rapacious noses. Ha, they will not know a thing about it for they will not suspect anyone working in that abandoned valley.

"If Jehovah, the God of Israel, will just help me even a little, I shall laugh at them and feed my family in spite of them. I know it is risky, but I would rather die defying them and fighting for life than to see all my family die by slow starvation. By the name of Jehovah, whom we used to worship, I will not submit in cowardly resignation to their murderous hatred. I shall defy them, their spies and even their fearful idols and gods. I, for one, will not bow my neck and obey their despicable decrees.

"This very night I will begin; I shall begin to pray every day to Jehovah, our old God of Israel. I shall ask for His help, and perhaps He will still hear us. I must confess I honestly don't know if He is with us or not anymore. I admit I am confused for I cannot accept the fact that, if the gracious and mighty God of Abraham and Moses was still with us, He would leave us in this humiliating and dreadful plight. Our aged elders have told us that Jehovah said that we Hebrews are His chosen people and He would never leave us. I really wish I could believe that."

That silent and solitary night — telling no one lest his secret somehow be found out — the young man Gideon of the tribe of Manasseh slipped silently away beyond the hills. He headed out through the ravines to the fertile valley he knew that lay hidden among the hills. Taking with him his father's oxen, he set to plowing in the cool night air with the vigilant stars as his only witnesses.

Gideon's Courageous Farming

All went as Gideon (for that was the name of that defiant young man) had planned in his hidden valley. No one discovered his secret efforts in the hidden valley. Apparently no spying Midianite detected his ripening field of barley. Every evening he walked anxiously to his hidden valley and each time the sight of the promising fields laid his anxieties to rest. Each day the fears plagued him, but each night a comforting green field awaited him. Even up to the very day of harvest he feared for he knew that his field was ripe for plunder.

At last came the longed-for day when his barley was ripe for harvest. Swinging his sickle rhythmically, he found himself humming an old song from Jehovah's Tabernacle. He slowly gathered his ripened grain and stacked it in sheaves for curing. So far all was well. He had seen no one enter his hidden valley; not even a man of his own people had wandered up there.

But the niggling fears would not go away. "Has some Midianite found it after all?" he wondered. Everyday he waited for the sun to cure and dry the barley for threshing. Gideon worried and fretted in his anxiety. "Would the Midianites wait till now, when my barley is ready for threshing? Will they sweep in and steal it all? Have they been secretly watching me all this while and will now come and kill me and walk off with my grain?" he apprehensively questioned within himself.

Gideon had worked hard and long in the night seasons and his well-ripened grain was almost ready to be threshed. While he waited for the grain to cure, he decided to hide himself in the brush at the border of his field. "I shall watch and see if some Midianite is about and my secret discovered. Fortunately, even if they do find this harvest, they will not know who has tilled these fields."

To his welcome relief the week passed most peaceably. He was overjoyed and thankful for such good fortune. "My family will not starve this year. So often I have cried out to Jehovah for deliverance. Perhaps He does hear my cries and has dealt kindly with me after all and has answered my prayers," he silently pondered this wonderful possibility. "Behold, I have a harvest ready to take to the threshing floor, and still no one beside me has come into this hidden valley."

The Place of Threshing

"At last all is ready," he said to himself. "Tomorrow I will take my grain to the threshing floor . . . to the threshing floor? Oh no, NO! I can't; I dare not go there. That place is always under surveillance; the Midianites will see me threshing there within the hour. With all the dust and noise of threshing, I will be caught before I am half done. I must not be so naive. I have walked carefully up till now; I must continue to outwit those sharp-eyed fiends. But . . . where . . . where . . . where can I thresh my grain and not be discovered?"

Anxiously Gideon wrestled futilely with his dilemma. "Where can I go to thresh out my harvest and not be seen?" he fretted. "If I am not careful, even one of my own people in their jealousy and desperation will betray me for that cursed reward of an ephah of grain." His predicament weighed more heavily on his mind as the week of waiting passed.

A Dream?

During the last night of his vigil, in a dream, Gideon saw himself threshing his grain in the old vineyard. In the long abandoned winepress that still stood under the branches of a big oak tree, hidden behind the newly leafed vines, he saw himself busily and tranquilly threshing his barley. When he awoke the next morning, his dream suddenly came vividly before him.

"That's it! Of course, that is the very place!" he cried. "The Midianites will never dream of looking there. Not only did they destroy all our wine and steal our grapes, but it is not the season for wine making. Besides, they won't allow us to harvest our grapes, so they would never think to keep the winepress under observation. It is three months before grape season, and no one goes there now.

"Ha, ha," he laughed in relief, "who would ever imagine anyone threshing grain there? No one ever threshed grain there, but after all, it is a nicely leveled place and the ground is well packed. For sure, it is small — definitely small for threshing — but it can be done and certainly no one will be watching that place.

"Hmm, I wonder, . . . could it really be? Did Jehovah our God give me that dream? I wish I knew. I really don't know, but I shall believe that He did. I never thought of it or never would have thought of it if I had not dreamed it. One thing is sure; it is an ideal place where no one would think to look. If there is any safe place, it is there."

The next night Gideon took the two oxen and carried his grain to the vineyard. "It will be crowded in that old winepress," he said to his dumb oxen. "It is really too small for threshing, but I know we can do it. Those cursed spies, they think themselves so clever. But this is one place those snoops will never think to look. This time I shall outwit them. I will! I really will have my harvest for the year!" he exulted. "It has been seven starving years since we could eat a good meal. Only Jehovah knows how we are still alive. But this year, thank God, will be different; we will eat and live.

"We have starved long enough. Too long we have fasted on husks and cooked grass and scoured the land to find morsels to eat. How long shall this go on? When will the time of sufficiency come, or better yet, the time of plenty of bread, corn, and wine? When will the sound of mirth, romping children, and singing swains come again to our land? O Jehovah, if it was You who have heard my prayers, given me this harvest, and spoken to me in a dream, I thank You. Please speed the day of our deliverance and revive Israel again."

But even as Gideon prayed his half-believing prayer, he knew that revival of the worship of Jehovah in Israel was indeed very far away. Moral decadence from the teachings of their false religion had so increased it was frightening. The altars and worship of the gods of the Amorites had become so popular to his people. Even in their misery, these idolatrous religions permitted and encouraged moral freedom from all restraint and licensed licentiousness in direct opposition to the laws of Jehovah.

2

The Question

Gideon was greatly encouraged with the wonderful idea the dream had brought to his mind. Without any doubt the old winepress was the ideal place to thresh his grain. Nevertheless, strange to say, the dream greatly troubled Gideon. Was it really true that Jehovah God had answered his prayers and had given him the dream? If so, it meant that Jehovah actually heard and answered the prayers of His people.

All his life Gideon had been taught and believed that Jehovah had left Israel after the death of Moses and Joshua, and no longer answered the prayers of His people. Jehovah was angry and had left them to their own devises. Besides that, He demanded such strict observance of His stringent law that the people had chosen easier gods to serve. In Gideon's day, Baal and the other gods and goddesses were the real divinities of the world.

Nevertheless, Gideon nurtured a hope in his heart that Jehovah was real and was truly King of all the earth. The stories of Israel's early history — stories of Abraham, of the patriarchs, of Moses, and of Joshua — had entranced him from the earliest days of his memory. There ever remained in his heart a certain belief in Jehovah, the God of Moses and of Israel.

"However, if Jehovah has answered my prayer," argued Gideon in his mind, "and He is the beneficent, all powerful

God of Moses, then how and why has He let His people come into such desperate straits?" His keen inquiring mind was caught up in questions and ponderings. Ideas he never before thought of bombarded his mind like hailstones on a warrior's helmet. Those uncalled-for thoughts shook the very foundations of the religious concepts he and his peers tenaciously held.

Those questions not only troubled him, but they also baffled him. "Why? Why are the chosen people of Almighty Jehovah — people that He had declared to Moses that He loved — living in such distressful circumstances? How can a beneficent God allow such lethal oppression and insupportable affliction to destroy a nation He claimed as His own peculiar people?

"Why do I have to go to such dangerous extremes and work all night every night to plant a field and harvest a crop? Why, if we are Jehovah's chosen people, must we precariously exist under the harsh dominion of the Midianites? They are a people that Jehovah never claimed as His people; they openly call Him their enemy."

"Midianites" In Hebrew Means *Strife*

Israel's conquerors, the Midianites, descended from Abraham by his wife Keturah. Generations ago they left the worship of Abraham's God and sank completely into the degradation of the idolatrous Amorites around them. They worshiped the fierce, wicked idols of the Canaanites that Jehovah declared to be an intolerable abomination to Him. The Midianites had totally abandoned all pretense of worshiping Elohim, the God of their father Abraham; therefore, they were under the curse of Jehovah for their evil customs and wicked idolatry. How then could Jehovah allow them to prosper, defeat, and persecute His own people?

Gideon wrestled and pondered the paradox of his situation:

... How could the Midianites, a cursed people, who were subservient to the Israelites for so many years, suddenly be allowed to prosper in their war against Israel?

... Why did Israel's God allow such wicked people to subjugate Jehovah's chosen people and torment them with such vicious brutalities?

... How could Jehovah, known as a merciful and loving God, permit such wicked persecution of Israel if He truly loved them?

... Why did He not arise in His power and destroy them like He did the Egyptians when they persecuted the Hebrews?

... How could He possibly bless such a wicked nation with so many favors and give them power to overcome His chosen people in battle?

... What could have possibly happened to weaken Israel and bring them into such calamitous circumstances?

... Was it true, as some old people said, that their Jehovah God abandoned them for their idolatry?

... Had their worship of the Canaanite gods invalidated the promises Jehovah had given to them?

... Had Jehovah repudiated them and replaced them with the Midianites; did He now cover their enemies with His gracious canopy of blessing?

... Were His mercies forever gone from the chosen seed of Abraham and would the Israelites no more be a nation on earth?

... Was there then no hope left for the tribes of Jacob to be succored in their troubles by beneficent Jehovah?

. . . Were the promises given to Abraham and Moses abrogated by Jehovah? And if so, when and where and WHY?

This Is Why

The writer of the book of Judges answered many of Gideon's questions in the very first sentence of the Biblical narrative, *"And the children of Israel did evil in the sight of the Lord: and the Lord delivered them into the hand of Midian seven years" (Judges 6:1).*

God had faithfully warned Israel long before, and Moses had faithfully recorded those warnings in his books. But young Gideon had never read or heard the admonitions God gave in the fifth book of Moses, because the books of Moses were old-fashioned and out-of-date. The Israelites were no longer required to listen to the reading of the five books of the law by the priests. In actuality, the priests had long before ceased reading them because they were too negative for the people. The people no longer wanted to hear them; in fact, they hated to hear them because hearing the law frightened them and pricked their conscience.

Only a few old folk remembered and passed some things on by word-of-mouth to their children. A few here and there still remembered Jehovah and believed in Him. However, in recent months many questions, arguments, and conversations had arisen about their God, Jehovah, whom they worshiped in days long ago. The story of Moses in Egypt and at the Red Sea still captured the imagination of the people at Passover time. More and more often it was secretly quoted by the old wise ones what Moses had written in his books:

"Moreover all these curses shall come upon thee, and shall pursue thee, and overtake thee, till

thou be destroyed; because thou hearkenedst not unto the voice of the Lord thy God, to keep His commandments and His statutes which He commanded thee: . . . Therefore shalt thou serve thine enemies which the Lord shall send against thee, in hunger, and in thirst, and in nakedness, and in want of all things: and He shall put a yoke of iron upon thy neck, until He have destroyed thee" (Deuteronomy 28:45,48).

God in effect had said, "I will deliver My people into captivity and take full responsibility for their calamity. Because they are My people, I will chastise them, as a man chastises his child, in order that they might learn to serve Me only, walk in My ways, and not worship the gods of the Canaanites. If Israel turns away from Me and serves and worships the false gods and idols of the pagan Canaanites round about them with the vile degrading practices I hate, then I shall not permit My people to presume upon My grace. I will take My mercy away from them and not help them any longer.

"I will teach them that My holiness and My laws cannot be violated with impunity. I shall show them the vanity and impotence of the idols they worship in My stead. I will show them, by painful reality, that the false gods of the Amorites and Canaanites are only myths and shadows. Behind those false images, deceitful devils work to destroy their nation. They shall learn the deceitfulness of those demon-idols. Pray to them all they will, those vain images cannot and will not help them, defend them or bless them in anyway.

"If I bring Israel into judgment and allow them to fall into captivity, in their pain and misery they shall call to their gods, but they shall not answer them, neither will they find in them any help or deliverance. Then in their distress they will remember My works of old and My delivering power to save. Then I shall turn them again to Myself that they no longer provoke Me to jealousy with their vile scenes of worship.

"Their abominable practices will become so common and universal, that everyone will be doing the same wicked things. They will no longer even consider them to be evil in My eyes. My people will think that I have changed my laws because they have changed them. They will assume that because what they do no longer seems evil to them, it is therefore no longer evil in My eyes. They will forget My word, and My law will no longer be obeyed. They will even presume to think I accept their wicked ways; impudently they will mix their obnoxious idolatrous rites with their worship of Me.

"Therefore, I shall chastise them in the only way they can learn. I will bring them into such trouble that they shall finally turn back to Me for help. And when they turn to Me, I shall deliver them again, show them that My love is constant and that My ways are ways of holiness. Furthermore, I shall deliver them in a way that shall convince them beyond any doubt that I, and I only, have delivered them. They shall not always be chastised, but I shall visit them and revive them as the summer rain revives the grass of the field and bring them back to life with Me."

According to His word, God left them in deep persecution until the purification of correction that He chose for them could do its full and perfect work. He waited out the time of their judgment till they would turn back to Him. Because He truly loved them, He did not allow His pity to terminate their sufferings. God determined to complete His righteous purposes. He would not prematurely intervene in His predetermined means to bring them out of idolatry and into repentance. He would not fail to bring them back unto worship of the only true and living God.

Israel's Response

When God determined to chastise His people and bring them back to Himself, He stirred up the Midianites to arise in war against Israel. To the complete amazement of the Hebrews, their enemies utterly defeated them. In one day the Israelites found themselves in the bitter woes of brutal captivity.

In their complacency before the battle they had said, "We are Jehovah's chosen people. God has given precious promises and cut eternal covenants with us. In our tabernacle we have the ark of the covenant where His Presence abides between the wings of the cherubim. We alone have the true chosen priesthood of Aaron; the glorious tabernacle of Moses abides in our nation. He will surely give us victory in our wars and battles.

"Furthermore, just in case, we also worship the same gods that our enemy-neighbors worship. Therefore, their gods will not be angry with us and turn their wrath upon us or help them to fight against us. Surely we have nothing to fear from the Midianites. After all, we defeated them soundly once before when Moses was still with us."

With but a few thousand men Moses had defeated the Midianites in battle many years before. In those days, when the Hebrews were obediently serving Jehovah, He made them a strong military power; ever since then, the Israelites despised the Midianites. They counted them as weak foes and held them in derision. They thought that because they had once routed the Midianites, they had little to fear from them. So the Israelites marched confidently into the battle convinced they could easily overcome them.

Why? Why? Why?

However, when defeat destroyed His people's presumptuous complacency, they pitifully complained, "Why . . . ? Why have such grievous circumstances been allowed to come irremediably upon us? Why are we, the sons of Abraham, Isaac and Jacob, forsaken by our Jehovah? How is it possible that we, sons of Abraham, have fallen into such woe? Why did not Baal help us? If Baal and the other gods would not help us, why then did they help the Midianites against us? We served Baal as well as they did! Is Baal jealous of the fact we used to serve Jehovah? After all, we have turned against our Jehovah in favor of Baal. Did we not placate him enough with our sacrifices and service?"

Recriminations

They wept in grievous lamentation, "We have lost our finest sons and husbands in the war. They lay like butchered cattle on the field of battle, and we dared not even bury them. Our possessions have been carried off, our homes vandalized, and our young women ravaged and carried into slavery. And we, like hunted hares in the meadows, must find caves and dens in which to hide for fear of their murdering swords."

Bitter, futile anger burned like acid in the Israelites' hearts against their cruel conquerors. They blamed Jehovah for forsaking them; they cursed their idols for not helping them in the war. "If we are Jehovah's chosen people, why did He let those who are His enemies defeat us and oppress us so cruelly?" they complained. "Much good it did us to placate and give offerings to the gods of the Midianites," they lamented. "They didn't help us any either."

They not only blamed God, but they also blamed their rulers and military leaders for their terrible plight and oppression. They said, "Our leaders told us that all was well and not to fear for our gods would give us the victory. Like fools we believed them and trusted in the gods to protect us instead of arming and training ourselves for war. We didn't make proper preparations, for we should have been better armed. This affliction has come because we have been too complacent and careless.

"And why, oh why, did we believe in the enemy's gods anyway? We know they are always full of deceit! The priests of their idols promised us peace and prosperity if we would worship their gods like they do; now look what lies those priests told."

Ten thousand *whys* echoed and re-echoed throughout their land. In every neighborly chat of the women at the well, questions and blame poured out of their lips. Whenever an Israelite met another in the field or on the path, hard and searching questions and lamentable blame filled the air about them. While they all asked lamenting questions, no one had any response with helpful answers.

It never entered their deluded minds that God would turn against His own people and favor their enemies — even though He had clearly said to Moses that He would turn against His Israel if they turned against Him to worship idols.

The subtlety of their idolatry and the deceitfulness of sin had so blinded their eyes and darkened their understanding that it never dawned upon them that the true cause of their misery rested fairly upon themselves. Their own foolish turning away from their wonderful Jehovah to worship idols, which they knew offended Him, had caused Him to withdraw His protecting grace from them. They had rejected the only true and living God and served the gods of the

Amorites with their vile rituals and revolting practices. In so doing, they lost His divine blessing and strong arm of help — there remained no one to help them.

3

God Begins To Work

"And it came to pass, when the children of Israel cried unto the Lord because of the Midianites, That the Lord sent a prophet unto the children of Israel, . . ." (Judges 6:7-8).

As soon as His people turned to Him in repentance and cried out of their hearts, Jehovah God responded. In truth, even before they cried to Him for help, God was beginning to intervene in their behalf. Anticipating their cry, God began to prepare a man with the right qualifications who would be His chosen leader to deliver them from their oppressors. Revivals begin with a man, not with a group or a crowd. God first chose His man; then He began the long preparation and development of his person, revelation and faith.

What, No Cry?

Why . . . ? Why had it taken Israel, His own chosen and enlightened people, seven long years of torment before they turned and cried to their Jehovah for deliverance? What was God seeking to attain by waiting seven years to hear their cry? Did not terrible cries and screams of pain and desperation rend the air from the very first day their defeated army let the ravaging Midianites pillage the people?

Screams of anguish, dying groans, shrieks of mortal pain and pitiful moans rent the air as thousands of Hebrew soldiers died from their wounds on the field of battle. Awful curses, horrible wails, and sobbed pleadings exploded into the night air as the pitiless conquerors pillaged the towns after their victory in battle.

Daily, pitiful moans of hunger and howls of pain from mindless brutality resounded on every side from the first moment of their defeat and down through seven interminable years. Forlorn cries of fear, sorrow, and pain, and ceaseless wails of lamentation with bitter complaints never ceased to assault the ears of neighbors and kin.

While their cries were pathetic to hear and their lamentable petitions to all their gods would seem to move the heart of stone, still there was no god that answered them. They had already turned from Jehovah to the gods of their neighbors, so their cries for help and mercy were directed to the Canaanite gods. While they blamed Jehovah for all their ills, they called on the gods, Baal, Molock, and Chemosh for help.

God remained ever attentive, yet none of those sighs or cries, groans or cursing was the kind of cry the keenly tuned ear of merciful Jehovah waited to hear. Not even the pathetic scenes of the wounded, the beaten, the shamed, or the captive slaves could turn the hand of Israel's true God to succor them. Not until He heard the *cry* He had long waited to hear, would Jehovah again move to help them.

Although it is true that revivals begin with prayer, it is also true that not just any kind of prayer will cause mercy to flow again. There are prayers that reach the ear and the heart of God; however, He will not hear or listen to just any string of words that someone decides to throw heavenward.

Right Cries And Wrong Cries

The ear of a mother is keenly tuned to differentiate between the various cries of her babe. There are cries that demand immediate attention and those which she can safely ignore. Israel vociferously cried out her pain and grief . . . remorse and fear . . . hopelessness and desperation . . . self pity and resentment . . . accusations and hatred . . . along with her anger and bitterness. However, such cries were not the ones that would enter into the ears of the faithful Jehovah and cause His hand to bring deliverance to His people.

His ear was attuned to one and only one cry; that cry His ear was ready to hear. Jehovah waited long to hear the one cry that comprised within it the ingredients that would cause Him to turn again Israel's captivity. That cry, the *right cry*, would show that His divine purpose had been fulfilled — that He had succeeded in bringing Israel's people away from their vain idolatry and back to Himself.

Holiness and Love eternally united with Infinite Wisdom and waited patiently for His people to recognize their need of Him and Him alone. *". . . therefore will the Lord wait, that He may be gracious unto you" (Isaiah 30:18).* God was willing to wait until His people would cry out to Him with the cry that would bring His immediate attention — the *cry of true repentance* and a decision to walk in His ways.

There are certain elements in prevailing prayer that God waits to hear before He will receive and answer the cry of His children and open to them the door of His heart of mercy. The cry that God will always hear must have:

. . . The low tone of humble confession of sin, failure and rebellion;

. . . The sincere sound of sorrow in repentance for the provocation of God;

. . . The sure note of faith in the divine heart of mercy;

... The sweet vibrations of praise and gratitude for the many blessings past;

... The deep base of justifying Jehovah whose ways are always right;

... The cheerful air of hope in Jehovah's mercy;

... And finally, the glad song of the will's surrender to abandon one's evil ways and idols, and return to serve, worship and obey Jehovah, one's own Creator God.

It took seven long years of chastisement for Israel to learn that Baal, Ashtaroth, and Moloch — the gods of the Amorites and Midianites — were but vain idols. Whether made of gold, silver, or wood, they could neither hear nor answer prayer. Dumb images, made by the hands of man, had no power at all to help. In fact, those idols were only a front for devils. *"...They sacrificed their sons and their daughters unto devils" (Psalms 106:37). "... the things which the Gentiles sacrifice, they sacrifice to devils, and not to God" (1 Corinthians 10:20).*

Israel also found it hopeless to try to save themselves by their own efforts. In spite of brave and arduous toil, they could not even reap a meaningful harvest by their own efforts. Their sheep, if not confiscated, were almost starved. Their cattle were weak and emaciated; their oxen too weak to do much work.

After trying every ingenious method they could devise, their efforts only came to a mocking failure. Any brave attempt to sow and reap a field proved futile and was terminated in grief when pillaged by marauding Midianites. Daily their impoverishment grew worse because of the malicious persecution of their enemy. At last, they resigned themselves to the fact that — with all their brave efforts and strenuous labor — they could neither harvest a crop nor live in their villages.

Seven long years. How long it took! How much suffering it required, ere they came to the end of all confidence in themselves or any hope in their false gods. When they remembered Jehovah as their only hope — that there was no other savior beside Him — then they cried out to Him to deliver them out of their troubles.

"If this keeps on much longer," they concluded, "we will be destroyed from off the face of the earth. Let us turn back again to Jehovah — the only God we know who is merciful and gracious. He is the only God that ever showed Israel any mercy or kindness. The Almighty Jehovah alone has the power to deliver us from the Midianites; at least we know He can if He will. He showed us mercy before with Moses and delivered us from the Egyptians in times past. If we cry unto Him, repent, and turn back to worship at His altars, perhaps He will hear our cry."

The wondrous faith-cry for mercy from a repentant heart arose first in one heart and then another. But as they shared their minds with one another, more and more they became convinced that Jehovah was their only hope. He alone had the power and mercy to save them. So little by little cry joined unto cry calling to Jehovah for mercy, pardon, and deliverance.

At first, many objected to a return to Jehovah. "He is a holy God," one said to another as they discussed their miserable plight. "He makes very difficult demands on us, and we all know how difficult it is to keep His commandments. We have already broken most of those commandments. That is probably why we are in these terrible circumstances. More than likely it was Jehovah that helped the Midianites and abandoned us in the battle. He is to blame for all our miseries, so why think that He would be merciful now?"

But the conviction that they must return to Jehovah gained ground as more and more said, "You are probably right that Jehovah ordained our defeat, but we deserted Him first. Truth is, we do not deserve mercy or help from His hands for the way we have abandoned and provoked Him. Besides, who else do we know who can deliver us? Have not our miseries lasted long enough?"

Slowly the detractors were out-numbered and their negative reasoning proved fruitless. Many of them also, under the pressure of misery, changed their minds until from all sides the consensus became, "Let us turn back to our Jehovah and cry unto Him for pardon and help."

God's chosen people began to remember His many mercies; all over the land a true cry of hope and faith, well flavored with the bitter herbs of repentance, arose in their hearts. Fearing, yet believing in His mercies, they cried to Jehovah — the only One they knew who was able to deliver them, no matter how powerful their enemy.

At last, Heaven rejoiced. The day God carefully planned and patiently awaited arrived. He heard the cry He had long been expecting. Out of their utter helplessness, they cried out to Jehovah with a cry of repentance, and that cry immediately reached the ear of their own true God.

As this cry grew in their hearts, the light of understanding also came to them and exposed their sin. God intended to reveal to them the true reason for their catastrophe. As they cried out to Jehovah, their only source of deliverance from their misery, they began to comprehend that their own foolish abandonment of Jehovah was the true cause of all their troubles.

One would say to another, "Did we not have peace and quiet, and were not our fields plentiful and our storehouses full when we served Jehovah? Were we not at peace and did not our enemies fear us as now we fear them? Have these vaunted gods of Baal been able to help us out of our troubles? We have sacrificed and faithfully served them according to all the prescribed rituals, but instead of delivering us they have only helped the Midianites against us.

"And has our life been any happier with the degrading morality taught by the priests of Baal? Our marriages fail; our children openly rebel. We sacrificed our children, our homes, our world-renowned laws of decency, our social structure, and our moral ethics for the same bestial lifestyle that our pagan neighbors practice.

"After all, in all honesty, who can show us that those vaunted gods ever once helped or blessed us? Was it not Jehovah who delivered our forefathers from Pharaoh and the vain gods of Egypt? Was it Baal or Jehovah that made us mighty conquerors over the Canaanites in the Revival of Deliverance under Joshua? Cannot that same Jehovah come and deliver us now?"

One by one they turned back to Jehovah. At home or in caves, in their walled towns and even at their tabernacle, they repented from their backsliding and their turning to other gods. They turned away from the practices of idolatrous infanticide and obscene fertility rites in the Baal-Ashtaroth worship. They repented that they had ever abandoned the ways of righteousness and begged pardon for breaking the laws of Jehovah.

So His people turned back and cried out to their own true God, Jehovah. *"And it came to pass, when the children of Israel cried unto the Lord . . . the Lord sent a prophet . . ."* *(Judges 6:7-8).* The prophet, out of his divine enlightenment, taught the Israelites why Jehovah's chosen people had been brought into such pathetic circumstances.

4

Message Of A Prophet

Deliverance for Israel was not to come by lightning from Heaven destroying the Midianites, nor by an earthquake opening the earth under their feet. God chose to bring deliverance to them by men: men of faith, obedience, and valor, ... men that were committed to God even unto death, ... men chosen out from among the Israelites in whom faith in Jehovah God still resided.

Deliverance from oppression was not the greatest purpose God desired to accomplish. He wanted to use this victory in the history of Israel for a higher reason than to merely liberate them from the oppression of the Midianites. He planned to bring a revival of faith in Jehovah and to deliver them from idolatry — from the pernicious bondage of their noxious fear of the pagan gods of the Midianites and their neighbors, the Canaanites.

Working patiently in the mystery of His own infinite wisdom and holy love, Jehovah answered their cry by sending a prophet to them. Through that prophet God revealed the true cause of their predicament and why He had allowed the Midianites to overcome them in battle.

This Is Why

Jehovah God wanted them to know that He was still their God, and that it was He Himself that had allowed the Midianites to overcome them. He wanted them to realize that He would not tolerate idolatry in His own people. They must recognize that He considered the wickedness involved in idolatry so evil that He, as their Father, would severely chastise them till they repented and abandoned it.

Not only this time but every time they rebelled and yielded to the enticing, lustful idolatries of the world around them, Jehovah, their God, would intervene from Heaven and chastise them. Because they were His own peculiar people that He truly loved, He would not allow them to be demoralized and destroyed by those corrupt practices.

After many years of silence the prophetic word of the Lord was heard again throughout the land of Israel. The voice of His prophet emphatically declared the startling message and succinctly answered all their confused questioning and endless *whys*. With one stroke of the sword of His word, God set the matter into clear light.

> **"That the Lord sent a prophet unto the children of Israel, which said unto them, Thus saith the Lord God of Israel, 'I brought you up from Egypt, and brought you forth out of the house of bondage; And I delivered you out of the hand of the Egyptians, and out of the hand of all that oppressed you, and drave them out from before you, and gave you their land; And I said unto you, I am the Lord your God; fear not the gods of the Amorites, in whose land ye dwell: but ye have not obeyed My voice'" (Judges 6:8-10).**

Jehovah plainly declared to His persecuted people that:

... the true cause of their many troubles was their rebellion against Jehovah.

... by turning to worship idols, they had rejected the God of Israel as their rightful King; however, He had not rejected them.

... their wickedness was so offensive to Him that He removed His impenetrable wall of protection from around them. Therefore their enemies, quickly seizing the opportunity, attacked and overcame them, and in their bitter hatred of Jehovah they mercilessly persecuted His people that:

... they must turn back and again worship Jehovah their own God and forsake the deceitful terrors of the gods and idols of their pagan neighbors.

... then and only then could He hear their cry and turn to His people in mercy and deliver them.

... He had not taken away His mercies from them, neither had He disowned them.

... He was the same Jehovah who brought them up from Egypt, released them from that house of bondage and set them free in the time of Moses.

... He was the One that had delivered them out of the hand of all their oppressors, driven out all their enemies from before them and given them their land.

Gently and clearly, through the prophet, He told them that He was the one and only God; apart from Him there was no other true God. All other gods were false; their promised blessings were nothing more than blatant deception and vain lies. He reminded them that He was the God, Jehovah, who had accompanied Moses and who, with irresistible power and marvelous miracles, had delivered them from the imperial power of Pharaoh.

With hopeful words, Jehovah lifted His people's faith and encouraged them to believe. He raised the hope they had abandoned in their agonizing persecution. Reminding them of His former powerful deliverance from a greater bondage, He encouraged them to believe that He was well able to deliver them again. Having delivered them from slavery and captivity in powerful Egypt, could He not easily deal with the far inferior Midianites?

In effect God told them, "I delivered you from the cruel bondage of slavery you endured under the hand of the powerful Pharaoh. I delivered you from the dominion of the Egyptian idolatries and from the tyranny of the most powerful nation of this world. I proved to you, as well as to the Egyptians, that their entire religious system and their pantheon of gods were all vain myths and malignant deceptions.

"I fed your entire nation daily with manna, and you never lacked a meal. I slaked your thirst for forty years with water flowing from the rock as I led you through the parched desert with all its dangers and enemies. Then with a strong arm I drove out the Canaanites from before you and gave you to possess the land in which you now live.

"Do you now say that the mighty Jehovah, Who overcame Pharaoh and all his gods, has lost His power? Is My mighty arm shortened that it cannot save? Have I not already proved My power and love to you over and over again? Am I not ready and able to deliver you now? Why do you say that I have abandoned you? Declare then, do you find fault in Me? Is it not your own sins and iniquities that have estranged you from Me when you abandoned Me, walked away from My fence of protection and turned to your own vain idols?"

God's word came as piercing light bringing truth to His people. His words were as true as finest gold and as penetrating as a search light — yet more tender than the sweetest song an angel could sing. God came to His erring and suffering people as the Ministering Comforter, the Spirit of Truth. His words, as fire, burned away the delusions of idolatry that, as a dark cloud, had darkened their minds from seeing truth.

He poured the oil and wine into their festering wounds. He encouraged them, built up their faith, restored their hope, and showed them the error of their ways. As a Father, He manifested His love and corrected them because He loved them.

Rays Of Hope Penetrate
The Darkness Of Bondage

The first prophetic rays of early morning light heralded the dawning of a new day; the Light of God's hope appeared on the horizon. God's people would not perish in their dark valley of pain under the harsh heel of the oppressor. Revival had begun in Israel. The voice of their Jehovah had:

. . . delivered them out of mighty Egypt;

. . . released them from the bitter oppression of slavery;

. . . cleansed them in the vicarious blood of the Pascal Lamb;

. . . baptized them in the liberating waters of the Red Sea;

. . . baptized them also in the fiery cloud of His glory and Spirit;

. . . carried them on eagle's wings through the desert unto a new land;

... led them into Canaan across flooded Jordan in harvest time;

... fed them with milk and honey and had given them grapes of Eshcol;

... and given them mighty victories over all the Canaanite kings.

Having done these wonderful works for His children, would their Deliverer now seek to destroy them because of their sins? No, instead He nurtured their faith and hope; He encouraged their love by reminding them of His abiding and eternal faithfulness. Remembrance of His many past mercies was like an anesthetic balm, a healing potion, that God poured out upon those that cried to Him with bitter tears of repentance.

The Fear Of Others — A Powerful Shackle

Jehovah had forewarned them not to fear the Amorite gods that surrounded them — those which their neighbors feared and worshiped. Fear of the false gods will always destroy faith in the true and living God. With those fears reigning in their hearts, they could never have faith in Jehovah. When the people of Israel began to fear the idol-gods of the land, they started their long slide down into apostasy and depravity.

Idols are false gods which have no power to help, and God had commanded Israel they must never worship them or have anything to do with them. However, they had listened to the cunning fables of their enemies and opened their hearts to fear the false gods; in fearing them they sacrificed unto devils and thereby lost their faith in Jehovah. *"They sacrificed unto devils, not to God; to gods whom they knew not, to new gods that came newly up, whom your fathers feared not" (Deuteronomy 32:17).*

Fascinated, they had watched their pagan neighbors placate the wrath of the gods they served. Apprehensively they had listened as the Canaanites described the deep fears they had of their gods and attributed all natural misfortunes to their supposed wrath. Also, all the natural blessings of rain or sunshine or other blessings they attributed to their sacrifices to those false gods. Little by little the people of Israel became contaminated by fear of the idol-gods and the more they feared the more they believed in them.

In their fear they said, "Those gods are powerful, wrathful, and vindictive! They are vengeful; they can do us much evil. They can either give us good health, fortune, and healthy crops, or, if offended, they will destroy our harvests." Fear transformed their faith into a fearful servitude of idols and unbelief in Jehovah. They doubted that their own true God could bless and protect them against the supposed power of the demon-idols. As the result of that fear, they fell to placating those man-made idols by serving and sacrificing unto them.

They brought shame to the Name of Jehovah, the true God of Israel, by raising up private and public altars to newly-made images in His place. They consecrated dark groves to practice evil and unspeakable forms of fertility worship. They raised up a vile priesthood from unsanctified men in their tribes. Slowly but irresistibly the idolatries of their neighbors usurped the worship of their own God. To their shame, they abandoned Jehovah's altar and raised up altars to the gods of the Amorites.

Gods Of Today

Today, in the so called enlightened twentieth century A.D., there are still deceitful pagan gods in the land. While their forms and names have changed, their characters, powers, and effective evils have not diminished.

Ashtaroth — the goddess of uninhibited lust and sexual freedom — still rules as queen of idols, as once the image of Venus in Athens, or Dianna in Ephesus, or Aphrodite in Rome reigned supreme in their shaded groves in former civilizations.

Molech — the god who demanded human sacrifice — today is the relentless pitiless god of commerce and big business that demands and feeds on human sacrifices daily.

Chemosh — the god of war and controversy — is secretly worshiped by many men of power who meet and plan acquisition of high gain as they bear sadistic and ego-maniacal rule over nations.

Dagon — the narcisistic god of self-love — has countless altars raised up to worship in self-gratification, self-determination, self-love, and self-rule! With his banner lifted high displaying proudly, "Please yourself, for you owe it to yourself."

Baal-hermon — the lofty god of arrogance and vanity, whose worship is as offensive as in yesteryear — has his golden god-shops of luxurious baubles located in every city in the world.

Baal-gad — the delectable god of fortune — has multitudinous hosts of devotees avidly serving him from Wall Street's board rooms down to the lowly book makers in taverns.

And who among the faithful idolaters of today are bold enough to refuse to bow the knee, pay tribute and render homage to Hermes — the god of fashion?

Besides these gods, there are a host of others — all "gods of the land" — that represent the worldly, flesh pleasing elements of modern daily life. They also demand faithful sacrifices.

Fear Not The Gods Of The Land

In the eyes of Jehovah, His people became stupefied with demeaning fear instead of filled with overcoming faith. They became abject appeasers instead of Flaming Believers. Rather than being free, hopeful, obedient, militant, and daring in faith, they became fearful, insecure, confused, uncertain, and divided. Their fears had transformed them into a herd of timid deer before a pack of cowardly jackals, instead of lions before the dogs of the idolatrous Canaanites. In their fear they retreated before the enemy — this was their evil in the sight of Jehovah.

When God spoke to them through His prophet, He opened their understanding — showing them how they had lost the former revival. He showed them the causes of their affliction. He also let them know that He was ready to work out the remedy and end their chastisement.

The Messenger

High in the Heavens the Almighty called one of His Angels and sent him to stand under a certain solitary oak tree in Ophrah near an old abandoned winepress. The Lord gave His Angel a special appointment with a specific word to a determined, confused but happy young man who would go there that morning to thresh his grain. The Angel of the Lord arrived first and stood comfortably under that oak tree; He waited patiently for Gideon to come and do his work. All morning He remained completely invisible to Gideon until he had almost finished threshing his barley.

🔥 5 🔥

A Strange Visitor

    The golden glow of dawn tinted the old vineyard as the first rays of light dappled the tops of the hills of Manasseh. All night long, for several nights, Gideon had labored surreptitiously with his flail beating out his precious barley in the cramped space of the ancient winepress. Threshing all that barley alone had been exhausting work, but at last it was finished.
    Just as the daybreak lifted the darkness from the earth, he finished threshing and winnowing his hard earned grain. It loomed lusciously before his weary eyes. That rich life-filled mound of golden barley was the finest, largest pile of grain he had seen in seven years. How enjoyable and soul-satisfying it was! He had defied the enemy, he had fought long and well, and he had triumphed in spite of the heavy odds against him. His reward lay piled up at his feet. Like a pile of gold it lay there almost as high as himself. Stuffed to overflowing with its promise of food for the coming year for his family, it was a sight to luxuriate in, to feast his eyes upon in blessed anticipation.
    Gideon congratulated himself for the bountiful supply of food he had gained and the clever way in which he had outwitted their wily conquerors. "I have plowed, sowed, reaped, and threshed my barley by myself night after night alone and in the dark. I have outsmarted the enemy. They are a lazy people; it never entered their heads to watch out for night workers.

"I am like that Old Terebinth, Old Solitary, standing there. That grand oak tree has stood alone for I know not how many centuries. All the forests about it were cut down long ago yet it stands. It has survived the storms of war and the weather; it withstood the attacks of woodsmen and fire. It survives as a symbol of a solitary fighter who refuses to be overcome, and it still stands alive and well in spite of its enemies. I can identify with the victorious aloneness of Old Terebinth; we both are survivors."

Thinking of that grand tree, the Terebinth — the Solitary One they called it — Gideon changed his position as he scraped the last of his grain together. Feeling somehow attached to the lonely tree, he looked up from his pile of barley to gaze affectionately at the old oak.

There, to his fright and astonishment, he saw a man casually standing under its great canopy watching him gather together his winnowed grain. "NO! OH, . . . NO!" he silently cried to himself as shattering fright pounded his benumbed brain. "Those clever, cursed Midianites have been watching me all the while, waiting till I had finished. Now they have come to confiscate everything I have harvested and to murder me also." In bitter sorrow his heart sank into the pit of defeat and despair.

At that precise moment the Visitor spoke to him. His voice was as pure as the morning sunbeams, as peaceful as the morning star that still shone brightly over his shoulder and as penetrating as a light shining in black darkness. As the sound of that celestial voice entered Gideon's ear, the horrid specter of fright immediately disappeared and peace enveloped his heart.

Never in his life had Gideon heard such a divine, melodious harmony as reverberated in that angelic voice. Its intonation seemed to wrap him in a mantle of peace and enfold him in waves of pure kindness. Its heavenly vibrations penetrated into his very spirit in blissful resonance and carried away his despair and terror as easily and softly as the wind bears afar the gossamer seeds of a thistle. Its renewing power revived both his spirit and mind as its soft soothing tones wiped away the weariness and the despair that had haunted him the last few weeks.

At the same time there arose within him a strange euphoric exultation that seemed to breathe a whisper of hope's revival within his breast. His whole inner being was suffused with glorious sensations he had never known before. He felt as if invisible celestial rays — radiating from the Stranger — penetrated his whole being and gave him inexplicable sensations of well-being and goodness. Nothing he had ever felt before compared with these new, other-worldly sensations that vibrated within his being.

The Messenger-from-the-Throne succinctly greeted him saying, "JEHOVAH IS WITH THEE, THOU MIGHTY MAN OF VALOR." The paucity of words was more than made up for by the supercharged meaning that filled each syllable. The Visitor spoke no more but continued to stand silently composed, waiting in celestial peace, and looking steadily at Gideon with a serene countenance that radiated love and tranquility.

At the invocation of Jehovah's name, Gideon knew immediately that his Visitor was not from the idolatrous tribes and peoples around them. With that holy and sacred name in His lips He definitely could not be an enemy. But then, . . . who was He? Where was He from? How did He find him in this hidden valley? How could He diffuse such a divine radiance about Him, seeing He had the dress and appearance of an ordinary mortal?

Obviously this unusual Stranger was not an Israelite of his neighborhood for Gideon was well acquainted with his neighbors. Furthermore, Gideon sensed within himself that this was indeed a holy man. How else could he account for the peaceful wonder of the Voice that had awakened such exalted feelings and had generated such wondrous exultation in his breast? The inexplicable aura of awe and reverence the presence of his Visitor awoke within him made shivers pass along Gideon's spine and gooseflesh arise on his skin.

Gideon could not answer his own questions as to who this Stranger was. However, one thing he was certain of, this man was not like any other man he had ever seen or known in his whole life. He completely forgot his pile of precious barley; his whole being was drawn into an encounter with this wondrous Visitor standing serenely under Old Terebinth.

God Had Seen, Heard, And Knew

God had seen Gideon's fears, hardships, and perseverance; He had listened to the cry of his hurting, questioning heart. Jehovah Himself had put: the determination to fight in his soul; the ideas of how to persevere in his mind; and the idea of the winepress in his dreams as he slept. Jehovah was well aware of Gideon's courage and tenacious persistence in growing and threshing his barley — indeed a daring feat due to the vicious persecution of the enemy. This feat manifested his own victory over his fears of the enemy. For had the Midianites discovered Gideon threshing wheat by the winepress, they most certainly would have killed him and confiscated his harvest.

However, Gideon had no inkling of the fact that his danger was really quite non-existent. Because Jehovah had chosen him to deliver His people, He had therefore carefully watched over Gideon, daily covering and protecting him from any enemy — man or beast — that might hurt him. Therefore, his courage and daring were valid facets of his character.

Who? Me?

His Visitor's extraordinary salutation astounded Gideon: "THE LORD IS WITH THEE, THOU MIGHTY MAN OF VALOR." Literally, "Jehovah is with you, O mighty victorious warrior." If ever there was a time when Gideon felt that such a greeting was a ludicrous exaggeration, it was now. Never before had Gideon lived in a darker hour, experienced so much fear or had his weakness so humiliatingly exposed.

"Oh yes, . . ." thought Gideon, "shout it among the people! Courageous Gideon hiding in the winepress because of his terror of the enemy. What can this Man possibly mean by declaring that God is with me? Why does He call me a mighty victorious warrior? Me? Gideon? How ridiculous! How incongruous are such words from this Stranger! He certainly must be a foreigner to these parts. But why in the name of Israel does He think that Jehovah is with me? Who is this Person? Where could He possibly have come from? Why has He come here to salute me? He addresses me as if He knows me, but . . . how could He know me? We have never before met each other; I am sure of that.

"Here I am secretly threshing barley while hiding in the winepress in abject fear to conceal my actions from the rapacious spying eyes of the Midianites. Me . . . ? A man of valor? A mighty warrior? That is really a bit too much! If I am so brave, what am I doing here in the winepress with barley and not grapes? To any logical observer this should prove that I am not overly gifted with valor and am deathly afraid of our enemies. I admit I would like to be flailing the heads of the Midianites instead of sheaves of barley. But barley I flail; this is no battleground. No indeed, such a designation as a man of valor certainly does not fit me."

"Thou Art, Because I Am"

But God — in His gracious dealings with man and in the light of His infinite wisdom, foreknowledge, and power — looks far ahead into the future to His finished work. He triumphantly declares:

... "Thou art Israel, the prince that prevails," to the scheming supplanting Jacob.

... "Thou art a mighty victorious warrior," to fearful courageous Gideon.

... "Thou art Peter, the rock," to unstable Simon.

... "Thou art Paul, the apostle," to the furious church-bashing Saul of Tarsus.

God counts a thing finished before He has even begun to work. Jehovah determined to make the man of His choice a man of such faith that he would dare to face and overcome the Midianites alone. He would make a man of faith and valor out of this plucky, daring, courageous yet fearful farmer named Gideon. Jehovah looks not for some experienced captain, nor a man of noble descent, nor even one from out of the ordained priesthood. God chooses a man, not for his natural abilities, but one that He can take in hand and make a *Someone out of No One*. God chooses an ordinary man that He will fill with His Spirit and revival fire; He makes him a man of God.

It is the artistic mind and skilled hands of the Master Potter that can take common clay and create a vessel of beauty and grace. Whatever ingredients the clay may have, it still cannot make itself into a vessel of distinction or great value. The Master Potter is not limited in His creating skill by the simple ingredients in the lump of clay. It is the masterful artistry and wisdom of the Divine Potter — not the drab morsel of earth — that makes an exquisite vessel of measureless value out of a bit of human clay.

6

Gideon's Searching Heart Finds An Answer

"And Gideon said unto Him, 'Oh my Lord, if the Lord be with us, why then is all this befallen us? And where be all His miracles which our fathers told us of, saying, Did not the Lord bring us up from Egypt? But now the Lord hath forsaken us, and delivered us into the hands of the Midianites'" (Judges 6:13).

Why? Why? Why?

The overflowing frustration of his thoughts, his mental confusion and his fruitless heart searchings overcame Gideon's awe and astonishment. Abruptly he answered his Visitor without even a courteous greeting. Bluntly he blurted out his frustration and anger to this amazing Visitor. "If, as you say, the Lord is with us, then, Why? . . . Why? . . . Why?" was the essence of Gideon's response to the Angel after recovering from his astonishment.

"Why has all this miserable suffering and ruthless oppression been permitted to fall upon our nation? Can He not see the obvious misery and devastation? Jehovah is supposed to be our God, but He has forsaken us and cares not that we are suffering death, famine, and deadly persecution. Does He even look upon our sick, starving, and impoverished people? Are His mercies withdrawn forever from us? Has He cast off Israel and taken the Midianites in their place? Is that why He causes them to prosper in all their ways? The Midianites never were His people; in fact, they abhor Jehovah and openly say so. Meanwhile, He helps us not at all."

At first, Gideon felt so confused that he really did not understand the message his Visitor had brought to him. The Angel had not said, "The Lord is with Israel," but pointedly stated that Jehovah was with Gideon — the man himself that God had chosen to use to bring Israel out of bondage. He was the man God had planned to transform into a conquering warrior of faith. But Gideon, in the blinding confusion of his own mental turmoil, continued to speak as if the Angel had said that Jehovah was with his whole nation.

Gideon continued his outburst, "Our fathers have told us that Jehovah brought us out of Egypt with mighty miracles. Where then are His miracles now when we so desperately need them? Has He used up all of His power and grace; is no more left for us? Was it only for the time and age of Moses and Joshua that He worked miracles? Is it true, as so many of my neighbors claim, that the age of miracles has passed? Is it true, as some teach, that the miracles of God were only for the beginning of our nation? Were Joshua's days the last days that Jehovah would miraculously intervene for us, His own people, and destroy our enemies? Are we now left to our own devises? If not, then why has He not intervened in our calamities and helped us against our enemies?

"Our aged men have often said that Jehovah was merciful, powerful and our own special Savior, but just look now upon our forlorn condition. Could things be much worse? Has He given us over to death? Are we so abandoned that we have no savior at all? Is His wrath so turned against us that He will destroy us? If so, why? What evil have we done?"

Give Me An Answer

"Sir, for long I have sought for an answer. Countless times I have prayed and cried to God seeking answers. My soul burns within me at our disgrace and destruction. We are the despised people of all nations! Doesn't God care that we starve, that many of our homes are abandoned and that our harvests are constantly destroyed? Does it make any difference to Him that many of our people must live secretly in caves and dens like miserable rats in cages to escape the hatred and swords of the Midianites?

"If, as we have been taught, Jehovah is all powerful and our national Savior, then why are His chosen people in servile bondage and worse than slaves? Must we stay in this state of misery and shame forever? Why are we Israelites, conquerors of Canaan, trembling in mortal fear like whipped dogs instead of shouting in triumphant victory?

"Stranger, do you realize all the cruelties and persecutions which fall upon our heads daily? If God is with me, why are my family and my people in such heartbreaking circumstances? Did Jehovah not see that this is the first crop I have been able to harvest in seven years? I had to toil in fear and trembling every long night. What do you mean when you say that God is with me? I have eyes and ears; I can see the oppression of my people. I can hear their cries of pain and bitter lamentation.

"Where are His streams of mercy that we were taught to look for in our own Jehovah? Sometimes I even wonder if it is true that He chose Israel for His own people and brought us out of Egypt to be a people for Himself. Is that but an egoistical myth of the Hebrews?

"Was our father Abraham really a friend of God or was he only a deluded religious fanatic? Was Moses truly empowered by Jehovah, or was it mere chance and good fortune that we escaped out of Egypt? I have believed what our fathers told us, but when I face the stark realities of our pitiable state, I cannot avoid doubting and questioning. Tell me if You know, O Stranger, is it only a myth of our forefathers that Jehovah, the Creator of the Heavens and Earth, is our God? Did He choose us for His people? Somehow I feel that You have mysterious knowledge that we do not have — that You have talked with Jehovah and have come to me.

"I hear these questions asked on every side by my friends and neighbors. As far as I know, one thing is sure about my time, I have only seen suffering, sorrow, and deep trouble. Sir, if You truly bring a word from our God, Jehovah, to me, tell me the truth that I may make peace with the bitter burnings in my heart. I confess that at times I have been so bitter and angry that I am tempted to die like a fool and rush out against the Midianites with my flail and ox goad."

Heaven Waits And Permeates

Meanwhile, the Angel, serenely tarrying in the calm and loving compassion He brought with Him from Heaven, waited for Gideon to unburden his soul. As He waited, divine rays of truth emanated from Him into Gideon's inner consciousness. Those rays of divine light radiating from His celestial Presence lifted long buried thoughts out of the musty dark corners of Gideon's mind and conscience, and brought them into sharp focus in Gideon's memory.

Without saying a further word, His heavenly Presence began to dispel the groping confusions of Gideon's mind like the early rays of dawn weaken the night's fortress of darkness. While Gideon kept on talking, little by little the bitterness of his soul was giving over to the rationality of heavenly truth and light.

Unsummonsed thoughts came slipping into Gideon's conscious mind and demanded an answer. "Yes, . . . yes it is true!" he responded within himself. "I know we have added Baal and Ashtaroth to our worship which Jehovah prohibited us to do, but they are such fearful gods. We thought we ought to placate them just in case. After all, one wants to be safe rather than sorry.

"Uh, . . . Oh yes, that too is true. I admit that sometimes I feel very ashamed of worshiping Baal. His ways are so contrary to the ways of our Jehovah. Admittedly, Baal's ways of worship are indisputably abominable. The rites of worship of Ashtaroth are certainly embarrassing and impure. In fact, I have often thought we worship them in vain. Our worship of those idols has proved utterly futile and worthless, for they have not helped us even a little.

"Blessed Stranger," continued Gideon to the Angel, "those idols we have worshiped come to my mind. Divine Messenger, I know thou art blessed for I feel thy blessedness radiating into my own soul. Tell me, please, is that the root of our trouble? Is our blatant idolatry the reason Jehovah has turned against us?

"Now that I think of it, somehow I remember that Moses said Jehovah is a jealous God and hates all idols that men call gods. Also, I call to mind the commandments that Moses left us which I learned as a child. He commanded us not to make or worship any graven images. Oh, yes, then it is true what more and more of my friends are secretly saying, 'Jehovah so hates our idol worship and because of it, He has left us!' Is that the true cause for our immense trouble?

"The old ones tell us there was a day when joy and gladness were songs in our lips and Israel rang with praise unto God. Is our idolatry the reason why our joy is all gone? Only sorrowful and bitter lamentation fill our days with melancholic refrains of our pain and torment.

"It is obvious that those idols are certainly not helping us any. But if Jehovah is with us, as You say, who then is helping the Midianites? Is it their idols whom they have always worshiped? Do their idols have power to help them only? Or is it that their gods are so displeased with us that we cannot placate them with our worship?"

Show Me The Way

"Where is Jehovah; has He hidden Himself from us? I would follow Him and obey Him if He would only reveal Himself to me. For somehow, Blessed Being, deep within my heart I know that only the great and merciful Jehovah is able to deliver us. Can You help me? If You can show me the way to Him, then You, who speak in His name, be merciful and tell me, I beseech You, the way to Him that I might find Him and discover His ways. My heart longs to see a real revival — Jehovah our God again abiding with us. I want to know the restoration of the pure worship of Jehovah. I no longer want to live under the fear of Baal and writhe under the shame of His worship.

"I simply cannot accept things as they are. Even as You stand before me, I seem to know that it is true; Jehovah is our God. He is true, powerful, and merciful. And someway . . . somehow . . . He will not leave us forever but will surely come and save us. O bright Messenger, as You appear to know where He is, ask Him to return unto us and cause us to return unto Him.

"O good Friend, I feel something so wondrously strange in Your Presence. My tongue is loosed to share my secret heart with You. Someway, I know not how, You inspire a new faith within me that I have never felt before. I do believe that our Jehovah God is eternal and changes not as Moses said. Is there some way that You can intercede for us? Oh, that I could find Him in my own day and not have to rely upon the stories of His past mercies from our fathers.

"A few of our oldest priests still try to practice a little of the same religious forms of old in our tabernacle, but frankly, they seem so useless and empty. The Shekinah Presence of Jehovah they tell us about has long ago disappeared from off our Ark as well as its cherubim in the Tabernacle. Where has it gone? Has Jehovah then also departed from us forever? If so, why? And where has He gone?"

Me . . . ? Man Of Valor?

"You salute me as a valiant warrior and tell me God is with me, but I do not understand how You can say such a thing to me. I have never fought in a battle in my life and know not how to use the normal weapons of war. I have never felt at all valiant, but when You greeted me just now, Your words entered into my ears and I felt an extraordinary rising of hope in my heart, as if our Jehovah had returned to us and would help us, so we could arise again and overcome our enemies.

"I certainly do not feel like a valiant warrior because I feel so helpless, so blind and so ignorant. Oh, how I wish I could arise in Jehovah's name against the enemy. Show me, compassionate Messenger of hope, how to return into the favor of Jehovah. I am as unenlightened as a child and know only the ways I have been taught.

"Behold Sir, the depths of my humiliation. If God truly was with me and I was a valiant warrior as You say, do You think I would be threshing out the grain and hiding in a place like this? If God was with me, would I be so afraid of the Midianites? Would I not have a large open field to harvest instead of that small field in the hidden valley?"

In My Father's Back Garden?

But even while Gideon spoke to the Angel, there flowed through his mind shameful graphic pictures of the idol worship in his father's back garden. Suddenly there flashed onto the screen of his memory in blazing letters of fearful fire the words of the law: *"Thou shalt have none other gods before Me. Thou shalt not make thee any graven image, . . . Thou shalt not bow down thyself unto them, nor serve them"* (Deuteronomy 5:7-9).

Gideon, as well as all Israel, were openly, contemptuously breaking God's Holy Law — broken and shattered commandments lay as accusing shards across their land. Their idol worship, so universally accepted, was a worship that everyone considered an acceptable and desirable addition to their long established worship of Jehovah.

In the light of the revelation that penetrated and stunned his heart, Gideon stammered into shamed silence. Suddenly he knew; yes he knew the truth — without his Visitor answering a single question he had asked. Gideon now knew beyond all doubt. Like a cloud — Divine light and revealing truth flamed fearfully into his heart — dark confusion lifted from his mind. He too had fearfully broken the law and commandments of Moses with their penalty of death. He too had deeply offended Jehovah with his flagrant idolatry. No, Jehovah had not abandoned them, but they had abandoned Jehovah.

Suddenly truth was clearing his mind. He knew, yes, he really did know the true answers to many of the whys he had so mindlessly and presumptuously asked his Visitor. He had accused Jehovah of his people's calamity. Jehovah guilty?

How dare he think such thoughts! No! No, . . . not at all! It was not Jehovah who had abandoned them and caused all their trouble. Israel's idolatrous backsliding had caused them to turn away from their own wonderful God and enter into the abominable worship and practices of the Amorite gods. They had made their own bed of trouble and now had to lie in it.

7

Gideon Looks Within

Gradually a sickening fear arose in Gideon's spirit and numbness gripped his mind as the dreadful light of truth invaded his inner being. It seemed like bright rays of invisible light emanating from that strange Being standing before him were penetrating into his inmost secret soul. In solemn silence he heard the inaudible voice of his own conscience demanding . . . questioning in the sanctuary of his own soul.

"Gideon, is it really true that you do not know the cause of all your troubles? Do you honestly think you can unilaterally reject Jehovah, the true and living God, and break His commandments with impunity? Do you really think that Jehovah — the God of Abraham, Moses, and Joshua — is deaf and blind like your graven images and perceives nothing about your wicked practices?

"Can you so deceive yourself by such rationalizing? Do you actually believe you may bow and worship the false gods of the Amorites and not provoke Jehovah, the living God of all holiness, to jealousy? Has He not made known to Israel that all idolatry is a repugnant abomination to Him? Has He not decreed chastisement upon Israel if they turn to worship idols and graven images? Can you sincerely say, Gideon, that you do not know why God has let the Midianites overcome and rule over you? Why is there no outpouring of divine blessing upon you and your people? Why is there no revival in Israel?

"Behold the rites and practices of your fertility gods. Do they not bring a sting of shame to your heart? The gruesome abominable offerings of human sacrifices those gods demand, are they not an anathema to Jehovah? Does He not hear the screams of agony of your babies as they are savagely sacrificed in the fires of Molech? Know you not that He hates such practices with total hatred? Come, tell me, can you conscientiously say that you do not know what caused the blessings and grace of your God to depart from you and your people? Do you know why you are all in such a calamitous state?"

"True, But . . ."

Gideon, finding himself justly condemned, tried to rise to his own defense and answer the accusing Voice within his soul. Vainly he offered excuses, "True, but everyone in Israel has idols in his house or backyard. No one thinks anything is wrong with idols. Worshiping idols is the popular thing to do even though Moses commanded us that we absolutely must not ever do it. Today, no one considers there is any sin in it; instead, everyone thinks it is the wise thing to do because we do not want those gods to be offended with us. Our teachers say that Moses' command was only for his time and not for today in our advanced state of religious development."

The Voice within his soul persisted, "But, is your idolatry the right thing to do, whether or not other people do it? Does the evil practice of others give you the moral right to do what you know is ethically, socially, morally — as well as spiritually — wrong? Was it Moses, or was it the God of Moses, who gave you the command not to make any graven image of a god or to worship any god beside the God of Abraham, Isaac, and Jacob, your true and living Jehovah?"

The Sharp Edge Of Truth

Dreadful conviction of his sinful state before a holy God seized Gideon. He knew in his heart that he was totally wrong; he had sinned inexcusably before Jehovah. Not only he, but all of his people had gravely offended their all-powerful Jehovah, who loved them with a jealous love and desired them for Himself alone. That strange irresistibly penetrating truth was cutting into his well defended conscience with a pain that was breaking his heart.

Comprehension that he had previously refused to accept and moral understanding he had not dared to try to decipher were lighting up within his soul. In spite of his desire to evade or escape those painful rays of truth, he could find no way to return to his former state of shadows and darkness.

Strangely enough, the very pain of his awakening felt good. It was as if some compassionate physician had come to him with hands of purest love and was lancing an abscess or evil within his spirit. He wanted it to stop, but he also found himself glad with what was happening. He also desired the process to continue until all the putrefaction found within him was all washed away.

Unexpectedly, Gideon found himself truly longing to be clean and to draw near to the God of holiness that had formerly seemed to be so frightening. He discovered a strange desire arising within his soul to have that same holiness that seemed to permeate the wonderful Visitor standing before him. Although he did not realize it yet, the spirit of true revival was beginning to awaken in Gideon's heart.

When The Lord "Looks Upon"

His Visitor continued to stand there in silence quietly looking upon Gideon with eyes of purest grace and holy light. His eyes seemed to look into the most secret depths of Gideon's soul. Gideon wanted to hide, but he knew there was no place to hide from the piercing eyes of holy love.

As the heavenly Visitor looked on Gideon, His eyes deeply invaded the secret heart of the man and saw the tormenting turmoil within. He saw the rays of holy light attack his ignorance, blindness, sin, and fear. He saw the confusions, his wrestling with fears and questionings. He saw the awakening conscience within his breast as the light of God shone there. He beheld the rising conviction of his idolatrous sin and the melting of repentance.

The Messenger from the Throne of Compassion also saw the hunger to find and know the real Jehovah God, the Holy One of Israel. The thirsting for God in Gideon's heart cried out for satisfaction. Those divine all-seeing eyes watched *faith* slowly awaken into life, as the light of God's Spirit quickened his heart — although Gideon himself was scarcely aware of what was transpiring in his spirit.

Old Beliefs Die Slowly

In spite of all the exciting, flamboyant feasts of idolatry and all the sorrow, pain and suffering of their captivity, Gideon had not yet totally abandoned his belief and confidence in the reality of Jehovah. He believed the reports the aged men often recounted of the Lord's marvelous acts of mercy and deliverance performed among His people. In his heart he knew the reports were true.

As a boy Gideon had eagerly listened to the old men as they had narrated the wondrous stories of their history: those thrilling accounts of the marvelous miracles of deliverance from Egypt, the many miracles Jehovah worked in the forty years spent in the desert, the exciting stories of the conquest of Canaan, and the incredible victories given to Joshua and his army as they marched triumphantly through the promised land.

Because Gideon had believed those stirring reports of Jehovah's glorious works in times past, a firm conviction grew deep in Gideon's heart that Jehovah could deliver them again, if only someway he could find Jehovah. As Gideon dumbly stood there in the Celestial Presence of the Angel of the Lord, the breath of divine mercy and grace breathed upon that quickened conscience and planted within his heart a *seed of faith* that would spring up into life.

"Go . . . , I Am With Thee"

The Angel did not directly answer even one of Gideon's questions, but even as he questioned, Gideon found that he already knew the true answers — he had refused to recognize them. The Angel answered him nothing concerning his questions. He watched as the Spirit of Truth shone His light into his soul, and, at the same time, He created faith in Gideon's heart.

Again the Celestial Messenger spoke to Gideon and gave him further light from God. His words had creative power within them to speak real faith into him and create a surety within his soul. The Angel gave Gideon a divine commission from Jehovah: *"And the Lord looked upon him, and said, 'Go in this thy might, and thou shalt save Israel from the hand of the Midianites: have not I sent thee?'" (Judges 6:14)*

What was Gideon's might? It was the divine word first spoken to him, *"Jehovah is with thee..."* In that Word God promised Gideon that from that day forward Jehovah had come to be with him; therefore, divine power and authority would accompany him.

Gideon's might was that wondrous Presence of God that was already at work within his soul. It illuminated the dark corners of hidden iniquity; it quickened the desire for cleansing and holiness. Before God could accompany Gideon in his chosen task, He must first cleanse and sanctify him and make him a vessel fit for God to use.

His "might" that the Angel mentioned would not be his own puny, fear-filled courage, nor his personal timid defiance of the Midianites at the winepress. The Angel meant that the all-powerful Presence of the Lord God had come to be with Gideon to deliver Israel.

Naturally, at that moment, Gideon was not yet sufficiently developed in his faith and understanding to go out immediately and fulfill God's mandate. Neither did he realize the scope and significance of the promise revealed in the Angel's commission. Nevertheless, God purposed to bring deliverance to His people and once more bring them out from their abhorrent idolatries. Gideon was the man Jehovah chose to work with to deliver Israel from the Midianites. As God's man, Gideon would be given the confidence that the Spirit of the Lord would accompany him. He would not go into that battle alone, but would go with the accompanying Presence of Omnipotent Jehovah.

"Go!" the Lord ordered Gideon. "No, not in your own small might, but go in the might of My Name and in the power of My Presence. Go with this understanding — your Jehovah God Himself, the great I AM of Moses and the Captain of the Lord's Hosts of Joshua, is with you. Do not be afraid or be dismayed at the power of the Midianites because from now on I am with you. As I overcame with Joshua, so shall I be with you.

"Go, Gideon, for you shall deliver Israel from the hand of the Midianites. Is it not I, Jehovah, the eternal God of

Israel, who has sent you? Your enemy will not be able to stand before us as I stand by your side in the battle. I will lead you, empower you, equip you and protect you. Though you are but little and helpless in your own eyes — full of confusions, fears, and questions — yet, you are the man I have chosen. Therefore, I shall deliver you and My people out of the hand of their oppressors. To you is given the privilege of facing the armies of the enemy together with Me, and we shall utterly defeat them."

God Is The Answer

The end and answer of the Patriarch Job's long search and multitudinous questionings was the appearance of God to him. Though God answered none of Job's questionings — God asked Job many unanswerable questions — yet, God Himself became the answer to all of Job's questions.

In the same manner God worked with Gideon; He never answered Gideon's many questions, but He Himself became the answer to them all. The one missing factor — the factor that alone could resolve all of Gideon's confusions — was the reality of the Presence of Jehovah. At last, Gideon had the answer to his long searchings. His God had come to him. So Gideon turned away from his small pile of barley in the winepress and stepped forth as the captain of God's army — a captain marching directly to the orders of Jehovah.

He had passed through long, arduous hours, days, weeks, and months of bitter struggles for survival. He had fought with questions, fears, and confusions because he truly thought that Jehovah had abandoned Israel. He had cried out countless prayers to Jehovah in case He might answer, but all of Gideon's strivings seemed to be unanswered. Nevertheless, in spite of prayers that seemed to be without answers, Gideon determined to do everything possible to frustrate the enemy and feed his family.

However, when the Angel of the Lord came to Gideon in the winepress with the living word of Jehovah in His lips, that word with its creative power, crashed through every barrier of doubt, confusion, and fear. It shot like a fiery infusion of truth into Gideon's heart. The empowered word quickened Gideon's whole being and created within his heart a faith that would grow until it would march fearlessly against the great military might of the conquering Midianites.

The Enemy Said . . .

Gideon was not the only one who heard those words of God that day. The Angel was not alone as He stood under the shadow of Old Solitary at Gideon's winepress. Ever keen eyes of the watchmen in hell saw that mighty Being of Light fly down to the ordered place under the shadow of Old Solitary. Infernal invisible ears from the nefarious regions of darkness drew near to listen to the words the Messenger from the Throne of the Almighty spoke that day. When those dark spirits, watching over their dominions, saw the Angel shoot forth from Heaven as a blazing comet straight to Gideon's winepress, the heinous horde quickly thronged around the Angel to hear His words.

The living words the Angel brought from the Imperial Throne thoroughly frightened those wicked imps and demonic rulers of darkness in the rebellious kingdom of Baal. Those evil visitors fearfully attended to every word of the message the Angel brought from the regions of light.

That divine fiat from the Throne of God, thundered horribly into the frightened ears of the unseen minions from the nether world. Those wondrous words that foretold the coming revival and deliverance of Israel struck deadly discordant terror into the ruling forces of malevolence that had gleefully and maliciously oppressed Israel through the Midianites.

With consternation they realized, only too well, that the declaration of the intentions of God decreed the utter termination of their cruel dominion over Israel. They knew their time of dominion would surely come to an end; they could no longer revel in the persecution of God's own chosen people. They clearly understood that, fight as they might, they would be overcome and forced to retreat in ignominy and frustration. Unless . . . unless . . . perhaps . . . what if they really hurried and arose in war before God could get Gideon and Israel ready?

Therefore, they rushed hastily back to the Midianites and incited them to put together an army immediately; they must quickly attack the Israelites before they could get themselves prepared. "Perhaps, this time if we hurry," they diabolically reasoned, "we can defeat Jehovah's plan. If we advance rapidly, we can destroy Israel before Gideon has time to muster up an army.

"We are not going to give up that easily," they schemed. "Even though Israel is repenting, it will take a long while — with all their idol altars — for them to get back into favor with the Most High. That will give us time to wipe them off the face of the earth.

"Why didn't we kill all the Israelites when we had the chance?" they moaned. "It was such an enjoyable sport to harass and torment them! We felt so sure that they were too far into disobedience for Jehovah to come to their help so we left far too many alive. This time we shall give no mercy or leave even one alive; we shall slay them all."

The rulers of darkness with their diabolical intentions to utterly destroy Israel before Jehovah could save them, rushed back to the chiefs and rulers of Midian. They incited them with their own panic — the fear kindled in them by the Angel's words. The rulers of wickedness from the realms of outer darkness persuaded the Midianites to send messages to other enemies of Jehovah, the God of Israel, to convince them to join together with them in a war of total destruction against the whole Hebrew nation. With such a demonic thrust empowering them, it did not take long to bring together an immense army of Jehovah haters. They immediately marched towards the borders of Israel.

"The enemy said, 'I will pursue, I will overtake, I will divide the spoil; my lust shall be satisfied upon them; I will draw my sword, my hand shall destroy them.' Thou didst blow with Thy wind, the sea covered them: they sank as lead in the mighty waters" (Exodus 15:9-10).

8

Not Impossible

"And the Lord looked upon him, and said, 'Go in this thy might, and thou shall save Israel from the hand of the Midianites: have not I sent thee?' And he said unto Him, 'O my Lord, wherewith shall I save Israel? Behold, my family is poor in Manasseh, and I am the least in my father's house.' And the Lord said unto him, 'Surely I will be with thee, and thou shalt smite the Midianites as one man'" (Judges 6:14-16).

Again, the Angel's faith-creative word from the Throne of God slipped into the heart of Gideon like a sweet zephyr from Heaven. As sweet waters from the springs of the eternal mountains, the ineffable Word revived his faith-parched soul. In that sublime moment, the immortal harmonies of that inimitable Voice captivated his soul. Celestial light, from that brief message from the mouth of the Angel, flooded his mind with God-given understanding. As a guiding star flashes a moment of hope through a storm-clouded sky, so also the Angel's Presence brought rays of understanding that removed the scales from off the eyes of Gideon's sin-blinded soul.

It was true! Heaven had heard Israel's hurting, repentant cry. Jehovah, Israel's own God, had deigned to grant mercy and speak to them again. And wonder of wonders, He was now speaking to him alone at the old winepress. The Angel's word quieted Gideon's roiling questioning and calmed his soul enough to hear what the Angel was saying. He heard, but still he could not comprehend its immensity.

"Who, . . . Me?"

"You mean, me . . . ?" he said within himself. "God is commissioning me? He is ordering me to be the one to arise and lead Israel into battle against the mighty Midianites, our conquerors and oppressors?"

In that celestial moment of impartation of faith, Gideon reveled in the glory and wonder of it all. However, after what seemed like a long while – when the shock of the Angel's words and Presence eased somewhat in his mind – Gideon began to realize and to analyze pragmatically the significance of those orders from Jehovah. In the reality of cold hard facts, it was an utter impossibility for Gideon to fulfill that divine commission. His newly implanted faith began to leak out of his heart like water from a cracked pot.

The celestial light emanating from the Angel did not cease to illuminate his inner being or to find the hiding places of his glaring idolatries and sins. Like an accusing ghoul, condemnation from his lately quickened conscience, indicted him mercilessly. What little confidence Gideon possessed slowly began to melt away like the morning dew when the sun arises.

"Wait a minute," Gideon reconsidered, "how could the holy Jehovah of Moses accompany me, such an idolatrous sinner, into battle against our enemy? Moses made it plain that God hated idolatry. Therefore, He must hate me, a self-accused idol worshiper. On the other hand, if Jehovah does not go with me, I would be a fool to attack that formidable army. But . . . , but the heavenly Visitor stated positively that Jehovah was already with me and would remain with me in the battle. His words sounded like inviolate truth when He spoke them.

"However, according to my past failures, lack of experience and very small resources," he reasoned, "how could I ever embark on such an immense undertaking? The whole idea is incongruous! Look at my pitiful poverty and lack of weapons. I have not a sword to my name! In fact, there is nothing that I possess or have access to that makes such an assignment possible.

"Honestly now, it would be ludicrous if it were not so dangerous. What a far out idea – to think that God should call me, a very obscure member of the most unimportant family among the hierarchy of Israel's ruling families. Who would follow me if I were to lead Israel to fight against that imposing host of the Midianites? Why, I belong to one of the poorest and most inferior families in the tribe of Manasseh.

"When I think of the awesome might and power of the Midianites, their numbers are mind boggling. I know there is no chance at all for me to overcome them. Everyone of them is fully armed with well sharpened weapons of war, and their hatred of us Hebrews is implacable. They won't leave a man of us alive on the field of battle. Furthermore, they are all trained and experienced soldiers while we are totally unprepared in every way.

"Me . . . ? Go out against the Midianites? How . . . ? With what army . . . ? By what means shall I save Israel? The logistics and cost of such an undertaking are prohibitive. My family is not a wealthy family with many houses; neither are we one of the influential people of our clan. I do not have any social or political influence to enable me to muster up an army. Furthermore, I am the youngest son of my father; therefore, I am the least of all in my house. How then can I possibly raise and equip an army without personal or family means?

"Where in all Israel are the hundreds of thousands of young men that would be naive enough to follow me into such a desperate venture? A large portion of our young men were killed in battle. Furthermore, from what resources could I draw to arm and train such a large number of warriors as needed to fight against the Midianite hosts — and that is not considering at all the immense task of feeding and caring for such a large number of hungry young men!"

The more Gideon pragmatically pondered the practicality of the issue, the more the sheer impossibility of such an undertaking possessed his mind. Natural reason asserted itself, candid rationality joined the issue and invincible logic took control over his thoughts and pushed his newly acquired faith into the shadows of common sense.

"Sorry, Sir, I Can't!"

Addressing himself again to his Visitor, Gideon said, "Sir, there has to be some misunderstanding. Do You realize that we are an occupied country and are prohibited by our conquerors to forge or make any type of weapons of war? Are You aware, Stranger, that we are weaponless and without any accouterments for war? The Midianites are a well armed and well trained fighting force. We are not only untrained, but our only weapons are our clumsy farm implements and tools. And added to that, they are not even sharp because the enemy will allow neither file nor sharpening stone amongst us. Besides all this, we are pitifully few in number for most of us were slain in the war.

"I could not conceivably be the person You seem to think I am. Shamefully, I confess my miserable poverty and painfully realize my total incapacity for anything so stupendous as the undertaking You have suggested. I am not a man of war, but a small ignorant untrained farmer. I have never used a sword in my life, much less could I be an army captain or commander. I am but a poor peasant with just enough to eat, thanks to this pile of barley. I cannot possibly run a war or wage a battle. There must be some mistake.

"Furthermore, contrary of Your opinion of me, truly I am of a very fearful disposition. If You really knew who I am, You'd know I am not at all a man of valor as You think. Somehow You must be mistaken; You think I am the one You are looking for – one valiant and aggressive. But venturesomeness, like You indicated, is not my personality; surely You must have some other man in mind. God could not have meant such words and humongous orders for me.

"I am truly sorry, my Lord; I honestly wish that I could do such a wondrous work. It would immensely satisfy my soul to take vengeance on our enemies that have brought us so much hurt. I would take much delight in liberating my people from such a plague, but such pleasant dreams are too high for me."

Meanwhile the Visitor from Celestial Shores, with His serene countenance unchanged, stood in imperturbable peace and calmly listened to all Gideon's excuses – He answered Gideon . . . nothing.

"Look, be reasonable, . . ." Gideon pled as fears grew within him. "In the first place, my resources are far too small to feed an army, . . . even if I had one. True, I have this pile of grain I had destined for my family, but it is far too small for any army big enough to overcome the Midianites. Really now, You are asking something impossible for me to consider. Much as I would love to see such a glorious victory, I just cannot perceive me entering into any entrepreneurial endeavor such as that. Please, Holy Sir, look for someone else who is much more capable than I – one prepared for such a great task."

But even as Gideon spoke to the calm, composed, non-answering Angel, his self-effacing excuses bounded around in his soul like a rubber ball in an empty barrel – empty that is of real truth. Even to his own ears his excuses began to have the ring of a false coin. Because God had planted the seed of faith by His word, it could not be uprooted by Gideon's weak arguments.

That seed of faith was already taking root and growing. His own heart began to silently deny his own words. That living faith in his heart compelled his reasoning mind to recognize that the Angelic word was true and indubitably true for him. Slowly growing in his heart, the seed of divine faith spoke softly but as clearly as a carillon from Heaven, "No, God has not made a mistake. I know that He has spoken to me; He has chosen me and called me to arise and wage war against the Midianites. I wish I could deny it, but I cannot. The truth is that I know, . . . although I do not know how I know, . . . nevertheless, I know God has spoken to my heart." And because of the truth of that silent voice within, Gideon accepted the word from God, but with much trembling. Still he inwardly sought someway to avoid the frightening responsibility.

"Your Ways Are Not My Ways"

Gideon's response to the Angel came out of his complete ignorance of God and His ways. He did not yet understand that the Almighty Lord of Hosts was not looking to Gideon's small resources to work out His deliverance of Israel. Jehovah purposed to deliver His people by His own strong right arm and was only asking Gideon to believe and obey – to be the human extension of His arm before the enemy. The Omnipotent Creator of Heaven and Earth did not need Gideon's small substance, natural powers, human might, or armies – nor did He need his pitifully small pile of barley.

God intended to work in such a way that Israel would know that Jehovah Himself performed the miracle of the awe-inspiring victory He would achieve. God would deliver them from the Midianites in such a way that they would realize that their God was mightier than all other gods they had formerly worshiped. Also, by His victory they would rediscover that He loved them and would deliver them – that they truly were His own people. Then they would turn away from the worship of the false demon-gods and return to their own true Jehovah.

Gideon's introspections and rationalizations only served to create doubts and confusions within himself and stifled his faith. Many fears of the consequences of failure arose in his soul. Gideon did not yet perceive the tremendous power and authority that resided in the DIVINE WORD which God had spoken to him.

"I Will Be With Thee"

Without entering into Gideon's logic and rationalizations, the Angel spoke powerful words from the Throne that answered his objections with a brief divine assurance that would strengthen Gideon's faith: *". . . Surely I will be with thee, and thou shalt smite the Midianites as one man" (Judges 6:16).*

In effect the Angel said, "It is not going to be you, Gideon. It shall be the I AM who accompanied Moses into Egypt, the I AM who opened wide the Red Sea for all Israel and the I AM who walked with Joshua around Jericho. I AM shall be with you. Therefore, with Me as your unseen partner, we shall smite the enemy as one man. We shall utterly destroy their armies, belittle their vaunted strength and laugh in derision at the power of their conceited gods. With you, Gideon, as My one arm, I shall break off the Midianites' galling yoke from the necks of My people and set them free.

"I ask not for the use of your small substance, inferior weapons, or your few followers. I shall use My ways, My means, and My weapons. Furthermore, I shall choose out My men to accompany you. What I ask of you is to implicitly and unhesitatingly obey My directions.

"Surely, I, Jehovah your God, will be with thee." This time the Angel's powerful words pierced deeply into Gideon's spiritual understanding. Those words, as lighted arrows from the Angel's lips, entered into the dark corridors of his shadowy fears and tore away the foundations of his dark rationalizations.

Jehovah reassured His chosen, fearful farmer by graciously repeating to him that he would not go alone into battle, not fight with his own strategy and not depend upon his own provisions. The Angel gave Gideon the true secret of the coming victory: namely, that the all-powerful Presence of Almighty God would go with him and he would not fight the enemy alone.

To God Be The Glory

God did not choose to raise up a self-sufficient, strong man with much weaponry in his arsenal and abundant means at his disposal. Neither did God will to use a recognized ruler of the people – nor an experienced commander of armies. Such a man would lean upon his own means, abilities and strength; he would take the glory of victory unto himself.

God chose not a wise man, a mighty man, or one of the nobles who would use his own resources and methods, and thereby frustrate God's plan to restore backsliding Israel's allegiance unto Himself. God looked for a simple, courageous man of faith who would move in explicit obedience — obedience even when it should appear to be folly and self-destruction.

God did not intend to inspire Gideon's faith, lift up his courage, give him weapons and an army, and then send him off alone to fight the battle. That would have been an easy task for God, but He desired to do something far more glorious. God determined to accompany Gideon with His own mighty Presence and go before him into the very camp of the enemy.

Gideon would fight this war accompanied by the invincible two-edged sword of Jehovah's Word and the irresistible shield of faith in his God. Unknown as yet to Gideon, trumpets would blast, . . . torches would burn . . . and searing effulgence of celestial light, like deadly lightning, would pierce the eyes of the enemy. God would so manifest His terrible Presence on the battlefield that blind confusion and panic and terror would utterly disorient the enemy in the betraying darkness surrounding them.

Deliverance would not come as the result of ordinary weapons in an ordinary battle. God willed an extraordinary victory that would not be won by force of numbers, military skill, nor the shock of dreadful fighting. Extraordinary weapons wielded by extraordinary faith in Jehovah would win the victory. Jehovah Himself would unsheathe His fiery two-edged sword disarming the heart and piercing through the flimsy courage of the enemy.

God planned to be ever present at Gideon's side as he faced the Midianites in battle. Not a single sword thrust would He allow to wound even one of the valiant few. The enemy could not come against the Hebrews because the blazing two-edged sword of the Lord would constantly flash between the two armies. That vaunted fierce Midianite army – so invincible by natural standards – would ignominiously fall in unrecoverable shame because Jehovah, the Man of War, would join His people in the battle.

🔥 9 🔥

Gideon Asks For Proof

"And he said unto Him, 'If now I have found grace in Thy sight, then shew me a sign that Thou talkest with me. Depart not hence, I pray Thee, until I come unto Thee, and bring forth my present, and set it before Thee.' And He said, 'I will tarry until thou come again.' And Gideon went in, and made ready a kid, and unleavened cakes of an ephah of flour: the flesh he put in a basket, and he put the broth in a pot, and brought it out unto Him under the oak, and presented it. And the Angel of God said unto him, 'Take the flesh and the unleavened cakes, and lay them upon this rock, and pour out the broth.' And he did so. Then the Angel of the Lord put forth the end of the staff that was in His hand, and touched the flesh and the unleavened cakes; and there rose up fire out of the rock, and consumed the flesh and the unleavened cakes. Then the Angel of the Lord departed out of his sight" (Judges 6:17-21).

With his physical eyes Gideon plainly saw the Angel from the Presence of God standing in human form under Old Terebinth, the oak tree. There was no doubt in his mind that his eyes were seeing a real person. His eyes were certainly not deceiving him. And not only through his eyes did he behold that Celestial Being, but also He could feel the inexpressible impression of blissfulness as that sublime Presence permeated his whole being. Added to the strong witness of his eyes and interior perception, his ears rejoiced in the harmonious melody of that voice – a voice so real and full of compassion whose loveliness so enthralled his being that he wanted to embrace it. But pragmatic Gideon still questioned the reality of this whole experience. So unearthly, so extraordinary, so beautiful yet so impossible, it was just too wonderful to be an actual fact in the real world.

But the message He spoke, Gideon could not dispute. That was too real to be some hallucination. Those words empowered by the exalted energy of that celestial Voice, pierced his consciousness and penetrated into his heart. As if they were sharp arrows of fire or shafts of pure light, they planted a faith in his heart that Gideon could not deny.

It Cannot Be True

However, even though Gideon beheld the form of the Angel, heard His Voice, understood His words, and received His message, still, everything that was happening seemed to him to be but a beautiful dream or an ecstatic illusion. His rational earth-bound mind told him this just could not be real.

"What is happening to me just cannot be true!" he reasoned. "My long nights of heavy labor and my unsettling fears have over-stressed my mind. This has to be some strange psychic phenomenon produced by too much wishing and mental strain. I have been under such pressure working night and day that I must be having some kind of hallucination. I see and hear things that are wondrously convincing; I love that sense of rapturous inspiration that fills my heart. Yet, . . . I still cannot believe that this unearthly vision is anything else but some strange vision and not a flesh and blood reality."

The divine command the Visitor gave was overwhelming to farmer Gideon. The challenge of leading an army into such a war, frightened, as well as challenged him. His Visitor was totally unexpected and undefinably unearthly; nevertheless, even in the glorious exultation of that exalted moment Gideon could not restrain the unanswerable, fearful doubts that bombarded his mind. They were like sharp distressing darts stabbing his reason. Apprehensions and misgivings flew about in his head like a disturbed hive of bees.

"I surely would hope this is really true. It would be exceedingly glorious if it were, but how can such incredible things be true?" Gideon questioned. "I must try somehow to verify it all and assure myself for certain. I must prove to myself beyond all doubt, that this is truly a visitation from Jehovah or only an overly-wished-for reality – a vain deception of my own heart and imagination."

"Wait, I Will Return"

Gideon felt compelled to ask an almost insulting favor of the Angel. "Please," he begged, "if it is really true that Jehovah has sent You to me, . . . and You – who are standing here before my eyes and talking to me – are truly an Angel from Heaven sent by God to give me this message, then grant me a miracle as a sign. Prove to me that you are who you say you are and are here in actuality talking with me. Wait here for me, and I will come again with my offering.

Suddenly and unexpectedly there flashed into the mind of Gideon a way to prove if this visitation was truly from

God; he would prepare a sacrificial offering. With the sacrifice of blood before the Lord, he would be able to appease this unexplainable sense of sinfulness that had so recently arisen in his heart. At the same time, he would observe how this most unusual Messenger from Heaven conducted himself before his sacrifice. "Sir," he asked the Angel, "depart not hence, I pray Thee, until I come unto Thee, bring forth my present and set it before thee.

"Surely," Gideon thought, "if I get away from this place back into the reality of my house, . . . back into my own realm . . . and out of this strange state that possesses me, I will get back to reality. Then, when I have taken time to prepare my sacrifice, He will have disappeared and everything will turn back to normal. Everything will be like it was before He came into my life. I will have a beautiful memory of an unexplainable vision, but that is all."

The Angel of God stood there as a living statue – amiable, immovable, and unoffended in the superior harmony of his own interior peace. With divine graciousness and patient benevolence He granted Gideon's request saying, "I will tarry until you come again."

And God Waited

Amazing condescension! Almighty Jehovah's heavenly Messenger tolerantly awaited a slow-to-believe earthling. The Angel, an eternal creature, subjected itself to time. Heaven condescended to wait for earth. What wondrous patience divine mercy manifested! Poor blind earthlings – ever so slow to believe – tried even the patience of Heaven.

It must have taken three to four hours for Gideon to return to his house, prepare and cook a kid with unleavened cakes, and then return to the Angel – plenty of time for

Gideon's mind to return to its normal earthly state and take refuge in his own environment. By the time his offering was ready, Gideon was quite convinced that it was all some hallucination or strange psychic phenomenon of his own overstressed mind. He was really feeling relieved in his expectation of finding the Angel gone when he returned; therefore, he would be free from such a heavy responsibility as going to war against the Midianites.

But God – ever forbearing, ever long-suffering with His people – was neither impatient nor repentant in His purpose. He would patiently work with His chosen son until He would develop him into the deliverer of Israel. Carefully, tolerantly Jehovah purposed to resolve Gideon's doubts, conquer his fears, and confirm His word. Jehovah would prove, beyond all possibility of some aberration, that this Celestial Messenger was sent from the Throne of God. He would effectively build up Gideon's faith until it would stand strong and certain.

The Angel Was Still There

Tentatively and hesitantly Gideon returned to the meeting place under the oak tree. There . . . oh, no! Oh, yes, . . . Gideon was torn between the two, for there awaiting him was that Celestial Visitor. He had not disappeared nor even moved from His place. Gideon was truly perplexed; he had not expected to encounter Him again. By then he had persuaded himself that this strange event was all his own imaginings. Gideon was perplexed, but not very surprised. For all his self-persuasion to the contrary, deep in his heart Gideon knew this experience was real.

Strangely enough Jehovah's Messenger was not offended with Gideon's request for a sign to prove His veracity and actuality. Angelic wisdom understood that God had unexpectedly commissioned a large task to a small son of Adam – this man dwelt on the forlorn sin-prone planet called Earth. He realized that His visit and words to Gideon, which were entirely unforeseen, would shock him with incredible astonishment. So, in serene patience He waited; Heaven's messengers are never late, impatient, or in a hurry.

God sent His Angel with orders to firmly confirm and establish the divine commission in the heart of Gideon. God comprehended the necessity of Gideon being made certain of the reality of this visitation and thereby become strong in his faith and acceptance of it before he could possibly dare to believe and obey such comprehensive orders.

The Sign Of Fire

In Gideon's day, fire coming down from Heaven upon a blood sacrifice was the unmistakable sign that Jehovah had accepted the offering. The proof Gideon desired to see was God's fire coming down upon his offering. The sign of fire from Heaven, unkindled by man, would establish full confirmation that this Visitor was genuine and real – not a dream or some fanciful illusion. With that proof Gideon could fully believe that a real living Angel from the Presence of Jehovah had actually come to him.

The Angel had neither requested nor even intimated that Gideon offer a blood sacrifice. His task was to build up the faith of God's chosen vessel to the point where he would receive and obey God's will. Divine orders to the Angel caused Him to patiently wait for Gideon to prepare his sacrifice; the kindling of divine fire upon the sacrifice would fully accomplish His mission.

Remission Through The Blood

Gideon's sacrifice was offered in the hope that God would be pleased with the blood of the kid shed for his sins; God would manifest His pleasure by sending fire to indicate that the offering was acceptable. This was Gideon's first sacrifice unto Jehovah.

Long before the Cross of Christ, God established that a blood sacrifice of certain prescribed animals was the only way unto forgiveness and cleansing from sin. Only through the shed blood of the accepted animal could Divine pardon be obtained. Even as today, pardon is obtained only by coming to the shed blood of Christ on the Cross.

When Gideon had the sacrifice all ready and the meat well boiled, he brought it unto the Angel, who by then had moved away from Old Terebinth and stood beside a large rock nearby. However, instead of sitting down and eating that kid with Gideon – as was the usual custom – the Angel commanded him to place his sacrifice upon that rock. (This indicated that the only way any offering or sacrifice of man can ever be acceptable in God's sight, is for it to be laid upon the Rock – Christ Jesus.)

Gideon had already boiled the offering on his own fire. Therefore, it was acceptable as an offering as it was and needed no more fire. However, the indisputable sign God would give him was to touch his sacrifice directly by fire without human kindling. As the boiled offering actually needed no more fire, it would be strong proof of His reality if the Angel brought fire out of Heaven.

Gideon placed his offering of boiled meat upon the Rock, but did not pour out the broth. Did he possibly think that he might be allowed to drink a bit of the broth or that he might even share some of it with the Angel? Or was it that he withheld the broth from the offering so as not to quench or hinder the fire if the Angel did bring fire from Heaven?

However, the law of the burnt offering required that it must be consumed by the fire of God in its totality. Because the law of the burnt offering required it be consumed by fire, it could not merely be boiled. The offering of a life unto God in sanctification cannot be acceptable if it is only a partially consumed (boiled) offering.

God would allow no part of the burnt offering to be used for human consumption. At the same time, the water of the broth upon the sacrifice would amply confirm the sign of fire that it was not some accidental earthly fire that a little broth could extinguish.

All Glory Goes To God

Man would like to keep a bit of the offered sacrifice – a bit of the glory, some of the rich juice of the meat, just a little gravy – for himself. Christ, poured out His whole being in terrible and glorious entirety at the Cross, and Gideon – who was a type of Jesus, the Deliverer of His people – was required to do the same with his offering. It must ALL be poured out on the rock.

Jesus withheld nothing in His great kenosis – the self-emptying of Christ. Not a drop of glory was reserved for Himself; He died without any honor. In the eyes of men, Jesus was a felon paying for his crimes of sedition and rebellion against the Roman government. To set His people free from death, the awful wages of sin, and to bring them into the fullness of life and pardon, it was necessary to pour Himself out without reserve upon the Cross.

When He poured out His precious life-blood on the Cross, John the beloved saw a strange sight. *". . . One of the soldiers with a spear pierced His side, and forthwith came there out blood and **water**. And he that saw it bare record, and his* *record is true: and he knoweth that he saith true, that ye might believe" (John 19:34-35).*

There came forth water as well as blood. The life of the flesh is the blood, and the life of God is the living water – both flowed out together towards man. Everything in Christ's sacrifice was consigned to the fire and flames of the Cross – both the lamb of sacrifice and the broth of all earthly glory.

Fire Out From The Rock

Gideon expectantly placed his offering on the rock in obedience to the Man's command. Then the Messenger extended His celestial staff and touched the flesh and the cakes. As the Angel's staff – which symbolized the Cross – touched the flesh of the offering, fire rose up out of the rock and consumed both flesh and cakes.

The fact that the offering had to be placed upon the rock before the fire came, foretold (in symbol) that the sacrifice of the shed blood on the Cross must first be offered before the fire from out of the rock can consume the offering. God thereby established (in type) the pattern of things to come. The Crucifixion of Christ on the Cross at the Passover had to precede the consuming fire of the Holy Spirit at Pentecost. Gideon (in type) celebrated first the sacrifice of the Passover, then the miracle fire of the Holy Spirit at Pentecost arose as fire out of the rock.

Gideon deeply desired God's fire as a confirming sign of God's Presence being with him. However, no fire could ever fall upon his offering before the blood was shed, which Gideon fulfilled before he brought it to the Angel. The divine order is first the blood of Christ for cleansing, then the fire of the Holy Spirit for the anointing.

Gideon fearfully watched this miraculous manifestation of fire coming up out of that rock. Meanwhile, while standing beside him, the Angel of the Lord who had touched the offering with his staff suddenly vanished out of his sight. Gideon was left alone standing in glorious amazement watching the divine fire consume the last bit of his earthly sacrifice.

The Baptism With Fire

The Messenger of the Lord had fully answered Gideon's request, even though He had now departed out of his sight. Gideon, at last, was fully assured that he had actually been visited by a real living Angel from Heaven. He wanted to shout, to dance, to cry aloud to the world. It was true! The visit from the Angel was no illusion but a real live Messenger from Jehovah. Therefore, every living word the Angel had spoken was absolutely true. The reality of it all thrilled Gideon's being with a glory he could hardly contain.

That kindling of fire by the staff of the Angel of the Lord, made Gideon a true believer. He walked out of his doubts as one arises and walks out of his dream; he marched into the realm of certainty and faith. He felt assured, beyond any possibility of doubt, that the Man who came to visit with him was the Angel of Jehovah. His fears, questions, and confusions of the last few hours disappeared; the fire had consumed them along with the flesh and broth of the sacrifice.

Gideon's spiritual mind was opened. With thrilling clarity he recalled the glorious Presence of the Heavenly Messenger, the One who commissioned him, encouraged him and promised him that Jehovah God would be with him. It really was true; Jehovah had come and called him to march out against the Midianites. Never mind how; God would take care of that, but he would obey and march.

At last Jehovah had answered his many cries and his urgent pleas. Gideon accepted – without any doubt – the divine commission for delivering Israel as his God appointed destiny. He didn't understand how he, a poor peasant farmer and a most ordinary man, could be suddenly commanded into decisive battle for the deliverance of his nation. That it was all true, he was certain. Although it was beyond his comprehension, it was not beyond his faith. God had fully established in his heart – as an inviolate and unchangeable fiat from the Throne of God – that he, Gideon, was chosen by Jehovah as the leader and commander of God's army of deliverance.

At last, God's impoverished people were actually going to be delivered from their terrible oppression! By faith Gideon seized hold of those living Words brought to him from the Throne. It was true. It was sure – as sure as the ashes on the rock before his amazed eyes. For reasons hidden in the counsels of God, he, Gideon, was chosen to lead the battle against the Midianites and deliver Israel from her captivity.

Gideon Believed

"No, Hallelujah! No," rejoiced Gideon as he looked at the still smoking rock, "I am not deluded. It is not an illusion nor a dream; it is not the result of an overly stressed mind working overtime. No, it is not my self-glorifying ego leading me into destruction. I have never in my wildest dreams had the desire to become a general of an army in Israel. I have too much pragmatism and know the impossible odds and the dangers involved for me to foolishly desire this directive of God for some self-glorying adventure.

"Jehovah, our own true Jehovah God, sent His Divine Messenger from Heaven to me to reestablish His covenant of mercy with us. He it is who has heard our cry and is come down to deliver us out from the cruel tyranny of our enemies. He has chosen me to lead, and with His help, I will.

"I feel like I have been reborn. Suddenly light has come into my darkness of unbelief. Those glorious stories our fathers told – of Israel's mighty deliverances by Jehovah in times past – were not just clever myths or fanciful legends. Our Jehovah God is truly the living God of today. He is real! He has and does manifest Himself to man. He actually was their Divine Deliverer, and now He has come down to deliver us out of all our oppression – to Him be the glory and honor forever!"

Gideon shouted aloud with exulting joy, "My prayers have been answered at last! My cries have been heard! Jehovah, Israel's true God, has come to us. We shall no longer be ground as chaff under the millstone of Midianite wrath. We are truly God's heritage; we shall be saved." And in the exhilaration of his fire-confirmed faith, he praised God ecstatically for His forgiving mercies and eternal goodness to Israel.

As this realization illumined his heart and mind, Gideon thrilled with the glory and wonder of it all. His faith in Jehovah was strong and daring. He didn't understand at all how God would give to him the victory, but one thing he knew – his God was real. God had spoken to him by His Angel and had chosen him to lead His people into victory. The revival glory rose up in his soul like a flaming sunrise after the long, dark night.

He had not merely imagined the Angel's visitation; behold the hot ashes still smoldered upon the rock, a sure material witness to the wonderful visitation from God and the divine fire from Heaven. Gideon's faith in God, in His Word and in His Messenger, took root as strong as the great roots of Old Terrebinth, Old Solitary. At last, in his heart Gideon believed God.

10

His Eyes Were Opened

"And when Gideon perceived that He was an Angel of the Lord, Gideon said, 'Alas, O Lord God! For because I have seen an Angel of the Lord face to face.' And the Lord said unto him, 'Peace be unto thee; fear not: thou shalt not die.' Then Gideon built an altar there unto the Lord, and called it Jehovah Shalom: unto this day it is yet in Ophrah of the Abiezrites" (Judges 6:22-24).

In spite of the inspiration and wonder of the Angelic visitation, Gideon did not fully believe his Visitor was an Angel from Heaven until He kindled the fire with His staff and vanished from his sight. Only then did the realization of what had happened begin to grip him. Yes, his Visitor was truly an Angel sent by Jehovah to bring him that special message. Such an event was so totally outside of his world that the significance of it did not easily penetrate his comprehension. Slowly he began to understand the immensity of his encounter.

For awhile Gideon remained in a state of shocked ecstasy. After the Angel brought fire out of the rock and disappeared, Gideon bathed his parched soul in the glorious afterglow of that Celestial Presence. Only dimly at first did he realize that his eyes had seen a real living Angel sent from God. Little by little the comprehension of that stupendous event grew in his soul.

However, as his comprehension grew it provoked in Gideon's mind a fearful and awakening apprehension. He remembered the rude offensiveness of his crass behavior – all the impertinent words of doubt, fear, and complaint he had spoken to that Angelic Being. What an enormous outrage he had committed to the Holy, Merciful Jehovah!

Jehovah had sent to him a holy Messenger from the very courts of Heaven, and he had dared to openly complain to Him. He had even openly questioned the veracity and goodness of Jehovah Himself. He had revealed that he doubted the very words that came from the Angel's lips. Now that it was too late, he realized that he had insulted his Visitor by daring to ask for a sign. The glory that had emanated from His Person should have been sufficient proof of His reality and the truth of His words.

The immensity of his unbelief and crude conduct overwhelmed Gideon. He fell upon his knees to the earth with a cry of anguish and fear. What would happen to him now? What punishment would be meted out to him from the mighty Jehovah he had so grossly offended? He was without any valid excuse. Gideon lamented, "Oh, if I had only been honest and spoken the truth to Him. I really did know, in my exalted spirit, that my Visitor was no ordinary mortal. How differently I should have spoken and acted! I certainly should have asked Him different questions. I knew He was from Jehovah, even as He said, but I did not want to admit it and expose myself. Oh, I acted with deliberate hypocrisy."

Gideon could not escape the memory of the interior illumination that flooded his being as he stood in the Presence of that Celestial Being. He still remembered the shame he felt as his own frequent worship of strange gods passed before his eyes. A series of shameful scenes of past actions in the grove of their idols had risen in his memory like evil specters. Intuitively he knew, without a further word from the Angel, the answer to his questions. He knew only too well why God had left Israel without help and allowed the Midianites to conquer them.

Into A New World

The light-filled words from the Angel, . . . the spiritual ecstasy that flooded his soul, . . . the blood sacrifice consumed by fire on the Rock . . . and the fire from the staff of the heavenly Messenger were like a Passover and Pentecost to his life. Gideon's eyes were opened into a new world; his ears unstopped to hear the ineffable Voice. In his newborn inner being spiritual perception and comprehension of divine things produced a new life for Gideon.

With his new spiritual enlightenment of the reality of Jehovah, there came also a dreadful fear of God into his soul. Gideon stood as one stunned; he felt himself nigh unto worthy of the sentence of death by the Eternal Judge. He had actually seen, heard, and talked with a celestial Messenger of the Most High God. A heavenly Being from the world of light and truth had come, and he had behaved himself worse than a beast of the field. In a suffocating sense of dread he cried out, *"ALAS, O Lord God, for I have seen an Angel of the Lord face to face!"*

"Alas"

Who can penetrate the depth of Gideon's word, "Alas"? Strangely enough, it is a love word of regret. A word meaning that one has offended another who loves him much.

Hidden away in this one word were bitter sorrows, as well as dread of the consequences of his recent rashness of behavior. His unbelief, his accusing questions, and his argumentative rejection of the Angel's message, now frightened him.

To make matters worse He had behaved insultingly to this gracious extraterrestrial Visitor. How could he have dared to question His veracity to His face? ". . . And me, with my own idolatry flagrantly practiced," he groaned, "I know idolatry is a mortal offense to Jehovah.

"How could I have been so blind? I deceived myself by thinking I did not know why our God allowed the Midianites to so oppress us. Really, I acted the hypocrite when I asked the Angel why Jehovah had left us, and why all these troubles had come upon us. As I stood there in His Presence, I realized that I really knew all the time but did not want to admit it – not even to myself. No wonder the Angel did not even deign to answer my questions; after all, He knew that I knew."

His shamed and guilty mind heavily accused him. His conscience told him that because of his reprehensible behavior toward the Angel and his sin before God, he would now fall under the hand of an angry God. Surely in His anger, the Almighty would slay him and seek out someone else in his place – someone who had more righteousness and faith, someone who had less unbelief and rationalistic arguments.

"Alas, . . . woe is me! What a fool I have been!" he cried. "I actually stood in the Lord's awesome, glorious Presence; like a dunce I openly expressed my doubts, raised my objections and babbled my confusions. Alas, I gave that heavenly Being no thanks, no reverence and no worship. I told Him I doubted He was really a true messenger from God. Oh, how could I have been so grossly offensive? I talked with an Angel of God as if He were another man – my own equal.

"Oh, what shall become of me? Will fire come out of that mysterious rock and consume me to ashes, also? O God, . . . I am worthy of death; I deserve Thy awful judgment! I shall surely die! I know it; I shall die for I have seen Your Angel face to face, and I offended Him to His face. I am a sinful man born in iniquity and worthy of all condemnation."

Ears Opened

Up to this time Gideon had unsuccessfully endeavored to comprehend the tragic problems of life in Israel. He had formed his opinions of life depending solely upon the reasoning of his own small intellect; his knowledge was locked into the philosophy of a wicked and erring society. He had tried to harmonize his meager knowledge of Jehovah with the chaos of defeat and oppression under which he lived.

This only awarded him with frustration and internal strife. The mysteries of Israel's suffering remained unsolved and far beyond his own powers of resolution. As his struggling and uninspired faith met the hard realities of life, Gideon found only confusing contradictions inundating his mind.

As a shipwrecked mariner contending with the relentless waves of the tempest, Gideon was sinking beneath the deadly waves of unbelief. He needed divine enabling to answer the *whys* of this brutal oppression of his people. Only Heaven could reveal the mysterious ways of God. Only faith could lead his soul to the haven of the rest and deliverance in God. But up till then, Heaven had always been silent to his cries. It was closed as if barred with impenetrable doors of brass; Jehovah was far away. As far as Gideon could ascertain, Jehovah apparently no longer talked with the sons of men.

However, when the fire was kindled on the rock, God opened the eyes and ears of Gideon's spiritual understanding. Gideon was thereby enabled to receive and communicate directly with his God. Previously Gideon had only understood things by the powers of his own natural mind. His small understanding was circumscribed by the petty world of a local farmer and illuminated by the dim glow of the ungodly superstitions of his people.

However, the Angel from Heaven had spoken to him and quickened his spiritual senses by the Word of God. Gideon's sins were now covered by his sacrifice so he could hear the voice of God speaking directly to his heart – his interior being. Before the blood sacrifice was consumed by the fire on the rock, Gideon's eyes were too blind to see and his ears far too dull to hear God's divine voice in his soul. His spirit lay dormant within him; it was as one dead or in a coma of frustration and unbelief. From that coma he could not arise unless God spoke the quickening word to his soul.

The life-giving impact of his encounter with the heavenly Visitor awakened his whole spiritual being. Therefore, it was no longer necessary for the Angel to remain with him visibly. Having "ears to hear," Gideon now could hear the voice of God speaking in his own soul. From then on Gideon entered into direct personal communication with his God; the Lord spoke directly to him.

Peace From God

The Angel was gone, and Gideon's fears were about to destroy his new found faith. God knew his chosen servant needed a rescuing word of assurance. Furthermore, Gideon also needed further revelation of the true character and goodness of Jehovah. He was already convicted of his sin and had come into the fear of the Lord.

Knowing that it was time for further revelation, Jehovah came to His repentant son with the kindest words the sinners ears can hear – words of grace and words of pardon. *"You shall not die, Jehovah Shalom is your peace,"* said that ineffable Voice within his soul. Into Gideon's terrified soul resounded the inimitable Voice of Jehovah. God spoke peace into his heart with transcendent words of divine self-revelation.

"Peace be unto you. Fear not, you shall not die." With those beautiful words of grace, God swept away his fears – swept them away as effortlessly as the hot wind of summer bears far away the downy thistle-seed or as the dawning rays of light banish the hateful fears of the night. Peace . . . God's peace . . . flashed with the power and light of creative revelation into his fear-darkened soul. God's words lighted the gloomy shadows of dread in his heart and lifted the weight of condemnation from his oppressed brain.

How gracious and merciful were God's first words to Gideon's newly opened ears: words anointed with the oil of gladness and perfumed with grace; words that opened a fountain of peace for troubled souls of all generations who might drink the waters of reconciliation with God; divine words from the Redeemer that calm the most terrified breast; words that are sweeter than the honeycomb, brighter than the midday sun, and more refreshing than the mountain streams in the sultry heat of summer.

"I AM PEACE; therefore, fear not, Gideon. There is no reason to be afraid. I have chosen you to bring deliverance to My people, not to destroy you. I am your God and come to you in peace. Be not afraid of My divine judgments and the penalties of My law. Because I accepted your sacrifice on the rock, your sins are remitted by the shedding of the blood of your lamb. At the altar on the rock I accepted your offering and confirmed it by fire. I am with you to help and shall make you My instrument of deliverance for your people.

I have not come to destroy you but to destroy your enemies and Mine.

"Don't be afraid of Me for I am not your enemy. I have never been your enemy. You turned away from Me and became My enemy when you worshiped other gods. I have only sought to bring you into deliverance and to show you My mercies. I sent My Angel: to bring you back unto Myself, to bring you into My pardon, and to bring you through My holy fires, into My Presence, because I truly love you.

"Fear not the gods of the Canaanites, Baal or Ashtaroth, Chemosh or Molech, or any other of the innumerable gods your enemies worship; they are but dumb idols that cannot talk, eat, walk or help.

"Fear not the Midianites, the Amalekites, their vast armies or their threatening words. They overcame My people because I was angry with their wicked practices and offensive idolatries. Therefore, I allowed them to overcome Israel and helped not My people against them. I am come now to be with you. This is My promise to you: *Thou shalt not die. Fear not for I am Jehovah Shalom. I am . . . Peace.*"

11

Jehovah Shalom

Jehovah Shalom . . . I AM PEACE. The glory-light of the revelation that God shone into Gideon's heart gave him a priceless gift of light. God gave Gideon a new covenant name of Himself – a name that He had never given to man before: JEHOVAH SHALOM . . . I AM PEACE! My nature is Peace. I always desire peace. I love peace. I desire peace in all My creation and in the hearts of all My children."

God took His Name, Jehovah (the covenant name He gave to Moses that revealed His I AM nature) and added to it the word Shalom (peace). Jehovah means He is ever constant, ever present, and never changes. Thereby He reveals that He is the covenant God of Peace and ever seeks peace for His people. He is Peace and will never change that attribute of His character. He is and always will be the God of Peace. He will always seek to come into peace with erring rebellious man.

This revelation of a new name of Almighty God brought the reprieve of Heaven into Gideon's fearful, self-condemned soul. "Hallelujah!" Gideon shouted to Old Terrebinth. "That name means that our Jehovah is not cruel or vengeful like the gods of the Amorites that so often brought fear into my life. Jehovah is Peace, and He is merciful. Our own Jehovah pardoned me . . . yes, me. Even though I am a sinner, I openly confessed to Him, and still He pardoned me. See, He is a God of grace and mercy. He is not vengefully bent on destroying me or His people Israel as I so greatly feared.

"He spoke peace right into my heart, in spite of my unrighteous ways, my unbelieving fears, my forbidden worship of graven images and my offensive behavior to His Holy Angel. Oh, my people, I have not really known what a wonderful and gracious God our Jehovah is. Revival streams of hope and faith have arisen in my heart. I can rejoice even before He brings deliverance from our enemies because I have found the truth concerning our Jehovah. Oh, wonder of wonders, He is Jehovah Shalom!

"We thought that He was an evil, wrathful God like some of our teachers told us He was. They became priests of the Canaanite gods and told us that Jehovah was too strict and demanded absolute obedience to His laws. They said that if we fail to observe His commandments – even in the smallest degree – then He would come, mercilessly chastise us and not pardon our sins. Therefore, we abandoned Him and chose other gods to replace him. We thought that by serving other gods He would leave us alone and not punish us; they would protect us from Him.

"But now I know that is not true, because He pardoned even my offensive sins of idolatry, my criticisms, and my accusations against Him to His Holy Angel. Now I know those teachers lied to us. He is just the opposite of the frightening vengeful gods of the Amorites. How mistaken we have been in our fears and unbelief to reject and abandon Him and to worship those foreign gods of gruesome aspect and evil character."

Gideon also understood by His new Name that God does not delight in war with all its accompanying brutalities. He never starts a war and is loath to make war. However, when His enemies start to war against Him, He will arise in war, and He always wins.

Jehovah Shalom hates all enmity; He is especially grieved when His own people arise against Him, resist Him, disobey Him and turn themselves into His enemies. He is Peace – peace is His nature and peace is His work on earth.

Jehovah, by the revelation of this Covenant Name, showed Gideon and His people that He is a merciful, peaceful, and peace-giving God. Jehovah, filled with loving-kindness, had come to bring peace to His people. He would take them out of their dark dungeons of fear into which their deluding idolatry had locked them. He would destroy their enemies who had destroyed them and their peace.

His divine Nature of Peace and good will towards men stood in marked contrast to the vengeful capricious nature the priests attributed to their Amorite gods – gods that ruled by fear and demanded sacrifice by threats of dreadful retribution. Jehovah Shalom, the God of Peace, shone as the full moon, supremely glorious, against the darkness of the midnight sky of false gods.

Necessary To Know God In Truth

Being fearful, sinful, and repentant, Gideon greatly needed to know the true nature of Jehovah. Without that knowledge he would not have the courage to lead Israel against the formidable Midianites. Gideon's awakened conscience and guilty fears would completely undermine his courage if any doubts remained concerning his own pardon and relationship with Jehovah. To go out to battle against an armed enemy thinking that one's own God is also your enemy is a certain recipe for defeat. Therefore, God revealed Himself to Gideon as Jehovah Shalom, the God whose nature is Peace. Gideon could only enter into the peace of pardon by Jehovah revealing Himself to him – while in a repentant state – as a merciful God ready to pardon his offenses and sins.

"Jehovah Shalom," Gideon marveled aloud, ". . . Jehovah Shalom, I Am . . . Peace. He comes to me in peace. Then I shall not die. He is not seeking retribution for my offenses or judging my trespasses. He comes to me as Peace, and I feel His peace rejuvenating my fear-dried soul as the spring rains revive the wilderness."

"I Am The God Of Peace"

"By His Name He tells me He is the God of Peace and assures me that I shall live and not die for my many sins. Therefore, He will fulfill His word, deliver us out of our terrible oppression and bring us to peace," reasoned logical Gideon. "I have gravely offended Him and insulted His Holy Messenger, yet He tells me that when I fight against the Midianites He shall go with me. I shall not die but live." Gideon rejoiced in the assurance of his faith. Jehovah Shalom would be with him in battle and bring him through it alive and well.

"Then we still are His People, and He is our Jehovah Shalom; therefore, our land will no longer be the arena of the cruel ravages and spiteful vandalism of our enemies. Israel shall again become the land of milk and honey. It shall be the land of peace watched over by Jehovah, the true Shepherd of Israel. He loves us, and in peace He has come to deliver us from our enemies.

"Once again, Israel will become a land of still waters and green pastures. Our fields, vines, and flocks will again flourish. This old oak tree shall once more see this abandoned winepress flowing afresh with the rich blood of grapes. Our starved cattle shall feed freely on the hills, and our fields shall give us bountiful harvest of wheat and barley. Those Midianites shall no longer plunder us at will.

"Our God, the God of Peace, has come to bring us into the welcome haven of rest. How His words refresh my heart! I hear His Voice singing the song of peace in my very soul, and like a river His peace flows through my spirit. He makes my feet to leap as the hinds in the hills for the very joy of such hope.

"The destroyer and oppressor shall be destroyed even by my own hand because the Almighty is with me. The Midianites shall perish; they shall fall as mown barley on the field of battle. I shall live and not die. The Midianites have come to war against our Jehovah. Aha! Their day is ended and the darkness of Sheol shall cover them. Their tyranny is ended; they shall oppress us no more. Our own God, Jehovah of Israel, has come to deliver us and bring us and our land into rest. We shall again be His people, and He shall be our God of Peace.

"Jehovah, Jehovah Shalom," sang Gideon as he leaped around the winepress under Old Terrebinth. In the joy of his revived faith, he sang in joyful anticipation of victory: "We rebelled against the Lord and rejected the God of Israel. Yes, we abandoned our God; however, God did not abandon us, but He enlarged Himself in our eyes as Jehovah Shalom. His mercies endure forever – even from generation to generation – they spring forth anew to bring peace with judgment. Jehovah Shalom is the balm of Gilead to the aching heart. He speaks words of life and pardon to the guilty soul. He said, 'I hate war and plunder, bloodshed and death; I will destroy the destroyer and bring Peace to earth. Return, return, O backsliding Israel, be reconciled to Me. Live no longer in rebel-enmity for I AM PEACE.' Jehovah Shalom revives the grieving heart, 'Peace on earth,' He proclaimed from the Throne of eternal Justice."

After his exuberance had subsided, Gideon continued meditating, "We willfully violated His righteous laws. We deserved our chastisement and received the painful rewards of our rebellions. In His justice He gave us over as victims to the Midianites. We abandoned our Rock, our Shield, and our Protector for the vain and powerless gods of the Amorites. Without Him on our side fighting for us, we were certain to lose the war. But our Jehovah, our God of Peace, has come to restore us to peace with Him and to establish peace within our land. Who is a God like unto Him, a Rock like our God?"

Gideon Worships

Gideon was meditating in relaxed peace; his soul was filled with gratitude and praise. As he worshiped the realization arose within him that he had never built an altar to God; he had never publicly worshiped Jehovah. He had been far too estranged from Him to ever worship Israel's true God. The altars at which he had formerly worshiped were devoted to the false gods they had borrowed from their idolatrous neighbors. With the wonder and peace from the pardon of his sins filling his soul, a deep desire came into his heart to build an altar unto Jehovah. For the very first time in many years, there would be an altar of worship of Jehovah in Israel. Gideon was becoming a man of God, and a true man of God will always be a worshiper. Revival fires were growing.

For as long as he could remember, Gideon had worshiped the Amorite idols at the altars raised up to unknown gods. In the lightened wonder of this revelation of Jehovah Shalom, the only true and living God, he immediately set to work to build an altar of surrender and commitment. And there, for the first time Gideon worshiped God in Spirit and in Truth.

For the first time in his life Gideon was enlightened as to the true essence and nature of Israel's God. "Truly," he said, " He is a wonderful God of love and mercy and truth and righteousness. No wonder Moses loved Him so intensely. No wonder Joshua served Him with all of his family as long as he lived." Gideon was beginning to understand how terribly misinformed and mistaken he and the people had been all this time.

God Of Peace, Not Wrath

Gideon had thought that if Jehovah ever came to them, He would come with the sword of judgment or some other instrument of the righteous wrath of justice. He would thunder forth His fiery vengeance like the terrible fires of Sinai. Instead, Jehovah's Voice was sweeter than the song of angels. His words more welcome to a repentant heart than a king's pardon to the condemned felon. His mercy was more reviving than cool wells of an oasis to the desert wanderer. "Peace!" Jehovah had commanded, "Be at rest! You shall live and not die, and together We shall smite the Midianites."

In the light of that revelation, all the tormenting, erroneous misunderstandings of many years was lifted as a dark veil from his mind. At last, Gideon knew directly from Heaven the true nature of Israel's Jehovah.

Over a hundred years had gone by since the death of Joshua. The light of the knowledge of Jehovah was fast dimming in the minds of God's people. Their idolatry and their resulting captivities had ravaged their concepts of Jehovah. The knowledge of Abraham's and Moses' God that still remained became twisted into a grotesque effigy of Israel's true Jehovah.

"No," Gideon contended within his mind, "it was not true what people have said. Jehovah Shalom has not abandoned us! It is the other way around. We left Him and adopted other gods; we left His peace and coverings." Therefore, the Israelites were exposed to the hatred of the war-minded nations surrounding them. Their distressing captivity was really not a mystery, but the logical result of their leaving their God of Peace and taking refuge under the canopy of the gods of war that their neighbors worshiped to their own destruction.

Gideon, set free from his false understanding of Jehovah God, could now understand so many things that had been such a mystery to him. Whereas before he had placed the blame of their troubles on Jehovah, he now realized they had brought their pains and sorrows upon themselves.

"Why did we deceive ourselves and think that Jehovah's ways and laws could be violated with impunity?" he wondered. "Moses and Joshua clearly warned us of the result of rejecting Jehovah and following the gods of the nations. Fortunately, Jehovah is a God slow to anger and ready to pardon when His people repent, for He delights in peace and not in judgment."

Although Jehovah had given Israel over to the tyranny of Midian, still He did not reject His own inheritance, His chosen seed of Abraham. Although He had administered chastisement in righteous judgments upon His children; nevertheless, He deeply loved and cared for them as a father cares for his wayward child. He was ready to pardon and deliver them as soon as He could bring them into repentance.

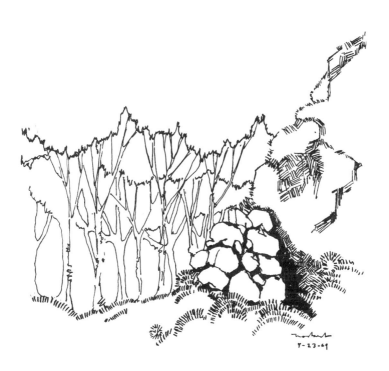

12

"Gideon, Clean Your Own Back Yard"

Gideon continued to bask in the euphoria of the glory and wonder of the grace and mercy that Jehovah Shalom had revealed to him. Suddenly he realized God was speaking to him within his soul, reminding him that there were Baal-gods resting insolently in his own back yard.

God had pardoned Gideon's sin and had brought peace to his soul; nevertheless, the idolatry in his life must still be faced and dealt with. God ordered Gideon to tear those altars down and to destroy them totally. Disobedience to this order, Gideon knew, was to lose his wondrous blessings of pardon and peace with God.

Mercifully, Jehovah had first revealed His pardon and His gracious disposition to Gideon, before dealing with his personal problem of idolatry. God needed to fully assure Gideon in his faith, before dealing with the basic obstacles that would obstruct his journey to full revival. His renewed faith would give him the needed strength to face and to deal with the deeply rooted fears that bound him to the idol worship that he had long maintained.

Being chosen by God as the deliverer of Israel did not mean that Jehovah Shalom would condone or even tolerate his idolatry. God did not give this assignment as a favor; He gave Gideon strict, direct orders concerning the destruction of his idols and pagan worship. He must utterly tear down the idolatrous grove, with all its accompanying images, before he would be sufficiently free from his fears and faith in those idols. It was imperative that the bondage of those fears be broken for Gideon to have the courage to face the Midianites who worshiped the very same idols.

It must be understood, that as mistaken and deceived as they are, idol worshipers believe fully that their idol-images represent truly powerful gods. Their gods are vindictive and vengeful in character and have ample power to severely punish offenders when their wrath is kindled.

"And it came to pass the same night, that the Lord said unto him, 'Take thy father's young bullock, even the second bullock of seven years old, and throw down the altar of Baal that thy father hath, and cut down the grove that is by it: And build an altar unto the Lord thy God upon the top of this rock, in the ordered place, and take the second bullock, and offer a burnt sacrifice with the wood of the grove which thou shalt cut down'" (Judges 6:25-26).

"Repudiate Baal Before Your People"

Before Gideon could defy and challenge the Midianite Baal-believers on the field of battle, he must first openly repudiate his own fear and faith in Baal. All Israel worshiped the false gods of Baal and Ashtaroth. This was the original provocation that caused God to deliver Israel into the hands of the Midianites for discipline and correction.

Gideon was told to overcome his own fear of idols and to cast down every altar where Baal was worshiped. Also, he must destroy all of the paraphernalia used in the worship of Baal and his consort, Ashtaroth. He must be the first to openly defy the powers of Baal before his own townsmen and personally prove to them the powerlessness of Baal to even defend himself.

According to battle customs of that day, the armies, when going into battle, would loudly cry out and call on the name of their gods for help; at the same time they would extol the virtues of their gods. If Gideon was not fully established in his faith, hearing the enemies' cries to Baal for help could discourage his faith and renew his fears of Baal. Those fears must be overcome and his faith well developed before God would lead him into the battle.

That very night Gideon must go – in willful obedience to the command of God – and challenge those false gods and their vain power. He must act in open defiance and publicly repudiate his former religion of Baal. Thereby he would show the local people that he had turned away utterly from worship and faith in those idols; the fear of them no longer possessed him. The result of this obedience would lift his courage to the place where he could face and conquer his fear of Baal. The victory over that fear would strengthen his faith to believe in Jehovah and to further obey His orders.

God planned that his obedience would reveal to Gideon that those gods he feared had no power to harm him or his family. He would be fully assured that those idol images had no life at all of their own. Fear of those idols had been instilled in Gideon's heart by his parents, his neighbors and the priests of Baal from his childhood. Now God would destroy those fears by one transcendent act of obedience.

Destruction of his idols would also openly declare to all the people that he had returned to Jehovah. It would be his testimony that his faith was firmly established in his own Jehovah Shalom; he had made an irreversible decision to believe in and to worship Jehovah – the only true God of Israel.

Casting down his own idols would also witness to both worlds, visible and invisible, the deceitfulness and the illusion of Baal's power. He would tear aside the curtain of deceit and prove that Baal was utterly powerless and helpless to defend himself from Gideon's defiant and disdainful destruction of his image. And if Baal could not even defend himself and punish his offenders, how then could he have any power to help or defend anyone else that trusted in him?

Gideon's Adventure Of Faith

Gideon immediately set to work to obey Jehovah's orders. He had talked with the Angel from Heaven and had lived. He had offered a sacrifice to Jehovah and had been approved by fire. He had received the saving revelation of Jehovah Shalom in his soul. Now his faith and assurance were sufficiently established to embark on a powerful soul-testing adventure of obedience. He would victoriously face his own powerful fears of Baal once and for all. If he died, . . . well, so be it, . . . but Gideon believed Jehovah.

"Then Gideon took ten men of his servants, and did as the Lord Jehovah had said unto him: . . . because he feared his father's household, and the men of the city, that he could not do it by day, that he did it by night" (Judges 6:27).

"Are you absolutely positive you are right and all of our neighbors, friends, and peers are completely wrong?" his fearful servants asked him as they were forced to join him that night in his labors. For at that time, everyone in Israel, bond or free, intensely feared the destructive and vindictive powers attributed to those idols.

Gideon had stayed strong in his faith; he believed they were all living under absurd delusion. In bright good humor he reassured his servants that all would be well because the all-powerful Jehovah was on their side. Jehovah Himself would prove to them that very night that the vaunted powers of those graven images were nothing more than unmitigated deceptions – deceptions invented by demons in hell and propagated by greedy self-serving priests who deceived the people by subterfuge and trickery.

"By The Power Of Christ, Destroy Baal"

The second strong seven year old bullock of his father, that God specifically indicated to Gideon, is a type of Christ in His overcoming might and power. For Christ is the second person of the Trinity, the beloved Son of the Father and the powerful overcoming Jesus of Nazareth. God did not expect Gideon to tear down the altar of Baal and uproot the groves with his own human strength and without strong help.

In reality, God was saying to Gideon that to overcome all the bondage of fear of idol-demons one must surely take Christ with oneself. With the help of His mighty power, Gideon would be able to overcome, to root out and to repudiate the idols, their fears and their abominable worship. He must work with the full authority and strength of Christ to destroy every vestige of demonic idolatry, as well as their accompanying obscene rites.

Gideon was not commanded to cast down his idols in his own power. Those brazen images, stone altars and rooted trees in the grove were too strong for him to push over and drag away in his own strength. They were too heavy and too well anchored for him to uproot. He needed the most powerful help available – the strength from the mighty second Bullock of his Father.

Only through the power of Christ, would Gideon have more than enough strength to tear down the idols in his life. In the unseen world the power of Christ, as yet unknown to

Gideon, would be at his disposal. By His Spirit, the powerful Son of God Himself would work mightily with Gideon to tear down the idols and uproot the shadowy groves that sheltered hidden sins. Christ Himself would uproot the great tap roots of fear and the tangled roots of lust that had rooted themselves in Gideon's soul, as he had worked in the garden's grove.

In the authority and power of Christ the Redeemer, Gideon would be well able to destroy the altars of Baal, as well as the ever accompanying groves of Ashtaroth. Baal and Ashtaroth were worshiped as the god and goddess of fertility and lust. Together they were the seducing and deceitful idols that fraudulently promised their devotees an abundance of harvest, and at the same time they threatened famine, war, and dire punishments for the smallest offense.

Every tree under whose shadow lust had lain and every image and symbol that had been raised to animate their devotees, had to be destroyed and thrown out. Every idolatrous representation of that defiling goddess had to be uprooted and burned in the flames of God's altar. Every idol altar, every form or ceremony of false worship, every tree and bush, every phallic symbol and all forms used in the fertility rites Gideon must overturn, destroy and root out. He could not leave a single bush standing behind which evil could hide. There must not remain the slightest fragment of Baal or his altar.

"Raise Up The Altar Of Jehovah"

After tearing down the altars and all that pertained to the worship of Baal, Gideon was to take the wood of those groves he had uprooted and cut them up for fuel. Then he was to build an altar to Jehovah and kindle a fire upon it. Following that, he must take that same mighty bullock he had used to pull down the graven image of Baal, slay it and burn it on the altar as a sacrifice made by fire unto Jehovah.

The shedding of that bullock's blood and the sacrifice made by fire from the wood of the trees was to be a cleansing, liberating sacrifice for all Israel – cleansing away the pollution of the Baal worship.

By this command (through types and symbols), God foretold of the sacrifice of His Son Jesus – the second mighty Person of the Holy Trinity – on the **wooden tree** of the Cross. Upon the Rock (Christ Jesus) God was building again His altar and renewing the rightful worship of Jehovah.

God said to Gideon, *"Build an altar unto the Lord thy God upon the top of this rock, in the ordered place, and take the second bullock, and offer a burnt sacrifice with the wood of the grove which thou shalt cut down" (Judges 6:26)*. With this command, God restored the altar of sacrifice in Israel. This would establish again the rites and order of sacrifice and worship Jehovah gave to Moses for the children of Israel.

The "ordered place" was the same place where the Angel had commanded Gideon to make his first sacrifice. It had already been sanctified by the fire that had consumed Gideon's first sacrifice. Probably, the fire the Angel kindled the day before was still smoldering on the rock. Therefore, it was fire from Heaven and not some strange fire of Gideon's kindling.

God did not send Gideon to the brazen altar of Moses at the tabernacle in Shiloh to offer his sacrifice, because Gideon – as deliverer of God's people – was a type of Christ, the Redeemer. To fulfill that type, God ordered him to offer his sacrifice upon a newly built altar based on the sanctified Rock. This signified that Jesus would be sacrificed on a cross on Golgotha, not in the temple.

Once again, the symbol of the Cross, the altar of sacrifice and the shed blood for the expiation of sin were established in Israel. There is not, nor can ever be, any other way to offer acceptable worship unto God other than by way of the altar of sacrifice – a type of the Cross of Jesus. Calvary is the top of that Rock; it is the ordered place that God commanded – the place of fire, blood, and wood placed in order upon the altar. It is the only place and the only way that true worship in Spirit can be offered acceptably to God.

13

Revelation Awaits Obedience

Gideon, whose name in Hebrew means, "he who cuts down," knew that his neighbors would take violent exception to his obedience to Jehovah. If they found out that he planned to desecrate and openly repudiate Baal, they would surely rise up as one against him. Probably they would stone him to death in the frenzy of their fear of Baal and wrathful vengeance.

The religion of any people in any period of history is a very fearful issue, because religion touches the deepest element of human nature. An undefined element in human nature borders on the spirit world for man. Religion attempts to give answers to the mysteries of life – be those answers true or not. Therefore, whether in Gideon's day or in our day, people can get very upset when their religion is desecrated, or worse yet, violently thrown down.

However, in spite of personal danger from his neighbors, Gideon knew that he had no choice. He had received and accepted the orders from Jehovah; he would obey them come what may. In his faith, he would neither fear the Midianites nor his neighbors. If Jehovah could lead him victoriously against a whole army of his enemies, then He could also protect him from a few unarmed townsfolk. Nevertheless, Gideon would not foolishly defy his friends and fellow townsmen or frighten them needlessly.

Therefore, he decided that he would work at night under the covering mantle of darkness. That very night, taking some men servants he could trust, he began to cut down the groves and to throw down the idols of Baal he had inherited from his father. There was no Angel of the Lord there to praise him for his courageous obedience; no neighbor came to strive with him for his religious fervor.

Gideon stood alone that night as he defied and destroyed his old fears and his former gods. Not a friend nor a kinsman was present to encourage him; he worked alone in his faith in his God. Gideon again typified Christ who alone cast out the devil, the prince of this world. Very often obedience to God will call for actions that must be taken alone; victories are won by men that stand alone with their God. *"I have trodden the winepress alone; and of the people there was none with me . . ." (Isaiah 63:3).*

By the help of the strong Bullock, working under the cloak of night, and with the ten strong servants to help him, Gideon fought his battle against Baal. Gideon began to chop down the trees and tear up their roots – roots of the short stocky myrtle and the leafy, bushy carob trees. It took many strong blows of his sharp axe to cut them all down. To destroy the grove, the altars, and the idols demanded hard determined effort and courage. All night he labored diligently to accomplish his task.

Gideon was not merely lopping off a few limbs to prune the trees of evil, for he had resolved to utterly destroy the whole evil, idolatrous system of worship his family had established. Every shading tree and every bushy shrub that provided concealment must be so rooted out that it might not spring up again come next spring. As quietly as possible they worked till the morning sky saw their work finished.

In the Scriptures nighttime typifies the time of Christ's absence from His Church for He is the Sun of Righteousness that was yet to arise in the world's history. In the darkness of history's long night – long before the dawn of Christ's return – axes chop vigorously, men work industriously and the Father's Bullock heaves and pulls, as obedient overcomers labor to destroy the idols in their back yard ere the Sun of Righteousness appears on the horizon.

Gideon, his servants, and the ox worked hard that night to finish the work of zealous destruction of Baal before bright dawn discovered their activities. Indubitably, as they worked Gideon prayed earnestly that all the noise would not awaken his brethren before he finished his task. (Obviously, that type of work could not be done noiselessly.) Jehovah answered Gideon's prayers and kept all the people sound asleep throughout the noise he made in his work . . . not a single neighbor, nor a member of his family showed up to disrupt Gideon's obedience. He finished the work before the sun arose in the east.

Gideon Overcomes His Fears

As Gideon was tearing down those idols in his own yard, at the same time, he also was uprooting all the tormenting fears he had suffered because of them in his own heart. He took victory over the fear of those graven images by his determined obedience to Jehovah's command. He would never more fear the power of those demon-idol gods of Baal. Gideon would not go out to fight against the Midianite army with fears of evil spirits and threats of their wrath and vengeance. Fearful threats they were that the priests of Baal and Ashtaroth brandished over the people to delude them and to have power over them.

The fear of his religious Baal-worshiping friends and brethren was another real fear that Gideon had to face and to conquer. The first enemy Jehovah must deliver him from was his religious kinfolk and neighbors. God had promised that Gideon would not die; he believed God even though his brethren might arise to lynch him. He trusted God to be his defence.

Enemy Brethren

How would his friends and neighbors react? What would they say? What would they try to do? They were his own people of the same tribe, denomination, beliefs, and idolatry. As Israelites they languished under the same oppression and captivity as he.

He understood that his obedience to Jehovah openly violated their religion and invalidated any or all help and protection those false gods were supposed to grant their devotees. Only a week previous to this night, he too would have been as angry as they. Had it not been for his encounter with that wondrous Visitor and the divine words now in his soul, he too would have reacted in violent fear and wrath.

He realized that he had offended them when he openly repudiated their god, their faith, and their teachings. He had dared to defy the demon powers of their gods and to build an altar upon which he sacrificed the bullock to Jehovah, whom the priests of Baal hated. Now morning had come; he must shortly face those same neighbors in their fright and anger.

Fear of man is a subtle powerful snare in life, especially to one who would endeavor to walk in obedience to God. This fear of man was the second battle Gideon had to face and overcome or else be defeated before he ever faced the Midianites. But Gideon believed the word of Jehovah-Shalom – that he would not die but live to fight against the Midianites and overcome them.

Morning's Startling News

That morning the news quickly spread in the village; the late risers awoke to a neighborhood buzzing with the cries and shouts of several hundred voices. All were crying out the shocking news, "Gideon has begun a revival of true worship in the ordered place on the rock. He has torn down the altars of Baal, overthrown and destroyed his image and cut down his groves."

In frightened panic and wrath, because they feared immediate retribution, his friends and neighbors arose against Gideon. They intended to slay him in defense of their false religion of idol gods. That was the only way they thought they might appease the wrath of Baal before he unleashed his wrath upon the whole town.

They had not received the revelation of Jehovah-Shalom as had Gideon. They were oblivious to the fact that their groves and their Baal-gods were extremely offensive to Jehovah and the cause of their own misery. Moreover, they were still strongly bound by their superstitious fears and their deluded belief in those false gods.

Therefore, when they became aware of what Gideon had done, they arose in violent antagonism against Gideon because he had uprooted and destroyed their established forms, rites, rituals, altars, and accessories of the worship of Baal and Ashtaroth. They were not about to change religions again and turn back to the worship of Jehovah.

Saved By His Father's Intervention

"And when the men of the city arose early in the morning, behold, the altar of Baal was cast down, and the grove was cut down that was by it, and the second bullock was offered upon the

altar that was built. And they said one to another, 'Who hath done this thing?' And when they enquired and asked, they said, 'Gideon the son of Joash hath done this thing.' Then the men of the city said unto Joash, 'Bring out thy son, that he may die: because he hath cast down the altar of Baal, and because he hath cut down the grove that was by it.' And Joash said unto all that stood against him, 'Will ye plead for Baal? Will ye save him? He that will plead for him, let him be put to death whilst it is yet morning: if he be a god, let him plead for himself, because one hath cast down his altar'" (Judges 6:28-32).

Gideon's fears had not been groundless, for as he anticipated, his neighbors rose up against him and cried out for his blood. When they discovered the past night's proceedings, they were terribly frightened and angry with the testimony of the revival of Gideon's faith. In this revival they saw the destruction of their whole idolatrous, Godless system under which they had groveled and worshiped in bondage and fear.

"Save our Baal at any cost! Let Baal live! We must slay Gideon for his terrible heresy," they cried. "Give us Ashtaroth! Give us Baal! Give us our fertility gods, for we know not if the imageless God, Jehovah, is yet alive or even the true God as Gideon claims. We want not our old God, Jehovah. We have never seen Him. How do we know He even exists? Furthermore, to worship Jehovah demands keeping stringent commandments and living a life of restraint, . . . certainly a pleasureless and dull existence.

"It has been so long since anyone ever saw Jehovah do anything for us; we only have the stories and myths of our fathers to go on. We can see Baal, and though fearful and vengeful, still the worship of Baal and Ashtaroth is pleasant. It gives us free reign to enjoy the pleasures of life without restraint.

"Away with Gideon and his Jehovah! He had no right to imperiously impose his religious beliefs upon us as if we were mere children with no right of choice. Give us our Baal and let Gideon die! Away with this impudent fellow! We have our rights to worship who and how we please."

Let Baal Arise

But even as his neighbors and friends cried out for his death, the God who had promised that Gideon should not die raised up a defender from Gideon's own household, his father, Joash, whose name in Hebrew means "whom God supports". In astute and supporting wisdom from God in this moment of crisis, Joash cried out to the angry neighbors: "Hear me, friends and neighbors. If in truth Baal be very god, if he has all the power attributed to him by his priests and brings swift retribution to his enemies, . . . then let him plead for himself. If he be as powerful and great as he is purported to be, let him save himself. Let Baal be the one to punish the man who desecrated his altar and brought shame to his name. If he is truly a god and not a mere stone from the quarry or silver from the smithy, as Gideon says, then Baal is quite able to defend himself without our help. In truth, this is a splendid opportunity to prove the powers of Baal.

"O mighty Baal," Joash prayed aloud in fervent prayer, "if you are really the powerful god you claim, then come and show your power against my youngest son, Gideon." But no thunder rolled, no lightning flashed, not a breeze stirred, and no shudder shook the earth. "What, . . . you do nothing to punish him? Perhaps you are afraid of him? Maybe you have lost your power to protect yourself? Could it be that you are too busy to care about your reputation? Perhaps you are sleeping or have gone on a long journey?"

As Joash mocked, taunted, and ridiculed Baal's supposed power, some of Gideon's faith began to enter into Joash. So much so that he joined the side of Jehovah and proclaimed, "It will take more than you, O Baal, to stop this revival of Jehovah. He is the God of our fathers. He is our God also, and we will have no other. Long enough we have slavishly served you, Baal! What good has it done us? Behold what dire straits we are in. It is time we realized our faults and returned to our one and true God, Jehovah.

"Let the man be put to death who shows so little faith in Baal as to believe that he has no power to defend himself and has to help his Baal slay Gideon! Why, such unbelief alone would be a terrible insult and desecration to Baal's vaunted power and vengeful nature. That is, of course, if he is a real god and sees what is going on," said Joash with deliberate irony as he ridiculed the religious zeal of his friends and neighbors.

"Gideon, my son, has utterly contemned Baal and violently destroyed his sacred altar and grove. Now let Baal arise and prove his power and authenticity to us with no outside help. Let mighty Baal alone by his own wrathful vengeance punish this impudence of Gideon."

Joash shrewdly turned the townsfolk's own misplaced faith, fears, and prides against themselves. If they laid hands on Gideon, they would automatically declare that their Baal was powerless to defend himself and thereby powerless to do any other work that he was purportedly able to do.

Frustrated Expectation

In fear and trembling the Baal-believers waited for Baal to strike Gideon to the ground in his wrath. They expected a thunderbolt to shoot out of the sky and slay him on the spot. Was Baal not a terrible god whom they held in mind-enslaving fright?

They waited and waited . . . and waited; but the only sign visible was the fire upon Gideon's altar calmly burning and its smoke ascending unto heaven . . . pointing them to Jehovah, the God of their fathers. The offering had been made in obedience and was pleasing to Jehovah. Meanwhile, Gideon stood by his altar worshiping Jehovah before them all and testifying of his encounter with Jehovah-Shalom.

Not the slightest stir or sign of wrath came from the upturned, smashed idol of Baal or his companion goddess Ashtaroth. Baal could neither extinguish one spark of that revival fire on God's holy altar, nor manifest in anyway his vaunted wrath against Gideon or his men to vindicate himself.

In his own revival of faith, Joash defeated the murderous purposes of all those deluded men; one by one they slipped away in shame and confusion. Pondering and questioning these strange things in their minds as they returned to their homes, they asked one another, "Is what Gideon said true? Did an Angel really come to him? Is Jehovah really alive? Is He no longer angry with us? Will He deliver us? Remember what that prophet told us the other day – that these Amorite gods are false and our worshiping them is why we are fallen into the hands of the Midianites. Are his words really the truth after all?" But no one was ready to answer. In amazement they all went to their houses considering all the wonders they had seen and heard.

Faith Begins To Revive

The shocking news traveled fast throughout the hills of Manasseh. "Gideon, the son of Joash, has defied and defiled

Baal and has remained unpunished and unscathed. Jehovah's altar has been built again, and the second bullock of his father sacrificed thereon. Baal, when challenged by Joash, could neither defend nor avenge himself. Where then are all his vaunted powers and mighty rulership over men?" the people asked one another. Strong doubt assailed the Israelites' hearts. Their faith in Baal and his power was fatally shaken.

"Can you imagine," they exclaimed one to another, "Gideon has disgraced and dishonored the gods of the Midianites with complete impunity! And he has restored our worship of old with his sacrifice to Jehovah on the altar. He has risen in faith and clearly declared that Jehovah has come to him and chosen him to arise and destroy the Midianites. Why, he even saw and talked to an Angel of Jehovah who caused fire to come out of the rock and consume his sacrifice. Some people have gone there to see; the ashes of that miracle fire are still burning there as proof."

These tidings were received by the Israelites with mixed emotions. Some received them with joy as faith and hope revived in their hearts. In their long misery and subjugation, they had grown weary of the god Baal who had certainly not helped them at all in their troubles. Many had secretly hoped to see the day again when Jehovah would return unto them. As the good news reached their ears, many began to praise the name of Jehovah who had remembered them in their misery.

Many took courage and faith; they went into their houses and tore down the god-shelves of Baal as their inspired faith in Jehovah rose into action against their idols. The powerless Baal could not take reprisals against a single one of them.

Yet, there were others that heard the wondrous news and reacted in fright and panic as the fears of Baal and the gods of the Amorites twisted their hearts into a panic-misery of fright. They expected that some calamity worse than they already had would fall upon them. However, their fears could not keep that startling news from shaking their faith in Baal; troubling thoughts came into their poor deluded minds.

Such stupendous news could not be kept secret very long from the Midianites. They were instantly alarmed when they heard that a valiant man had arisen in Israel and had desecrated their Amorite gods with impunity. They were astounded and very upset when they found out that he had also raised again the altar of Jehovah. Immediately they determined they must quickly arise to destroy Gideon at once — destroy him before he could form an army or before his terrible Jehovah God could help Israel. All too well they remembered the exploits of Jehovah for His people in former times. They themselves had been soundly defeated by that God, Jehovah, in the time of Moses. They were not about to allow a revival of the worship of Jehovah to rise again in Israel.

Stop The Revival Quick

In their fear of Jehovah, the Midianites hastily sent to the Amalekites (one of the tribes of Esau) to come and help them. But then they feared that even the Amalekites were not enough help. Their fear of Jehovah was so unnerving that they persuaded the Amorites (whose gods had been so vilified by Gideon) to join with them. They knew they must again subdue Israel and force them to return to Baal before the revival of Jehovah worship could gather strength.

"Come and help us," they insisted. "Gideon has restored the worship of Jehovah in Israel. They are in a glorious revival of faith and hope. They have contemptuously thrown out our Baal god; they claim he is vain and helpless." With this news, their Amalekite and Edomite neighbors in great fright hastily gathered their armies together for war.

These three armies quickly gathered together and marched to the valley of Jezreel (which means "God scatters"). Was it by chance that they chose a valley with this particular name? They intended to fight against Israel and Gideon – to bring them into submission and to stop the revival before it could bring deliverance to Israel.

Little did those Midianites know that God had already begun deliverance; the revival was already taking hold in the hearts of His people. Already God had delivered Gideon from his sins, from his fears, and from his idolatry. And with him many others had taken courage and followed the footsteps of Gideon. Three armies together could never stop that revival in Israel.

Sin is the substance that gives power to the devil and his hosts over the people of God. Therefore, when God could bring His people into repentance and cleansing from their sin in the shed blood of the sacrifice, Israel was already coming under the banner of Jehovah Nissi, the Lord our Banner. Revival fires had already begun to burn and nothing the enemy could do could stop it. If the Midianite's army had been twice its size, it was still too little and too late.

That large heathen horde joined together for one purpose only and that was to destroy Gideon – the man of God who had arisen in the name of Jehovah – and to wipe out his revival of faith in Jehovah. They knew they must act quickly before he had time to form his army, train his soldiers, and prepare his weapons for battle. For if they delayed, they would allow the God of Israel to be joined again with His people.

Gideon had not yet called together an army. He was but one man of obscure name and fame in Israel, yet three powerful nations joined their armies together to slay him. What immeasurable fear they had of Israel's Jehovah! And oh, how well that fear was founded! Because when they had been so defeated and destroyed by the God of Israel before, it had taken them centuries to recover. They were not taking any chances again against that mighty Jehovah God of the Israelites.

The Mighty Victor

Gideon delivering Israel from the Midianite army typifies Jesus Christ – the mighty Victor and Champion of His people. First of all, Christ Jesus, Jehovah in flesh, overcame the demon-idols of the lust of the flesh, the lust of the eyes, and the pride of life. There on the battlefield in the wilderness of Judea, He met the devil, the champion of evil, and the wily tempter, in person.

Then, in obedience to God, Jesus – in His faith in the promises of God – attacked and tore down the religious superstitions and false teachings of His day. And in so doing He infuriated His neighbors and fellow citizens of Judea causing them to rise up in vindictive hate to slay Him.

They set upon Jesus as they set upon Gideon, desiring to slay Him for destroying their popular beliefs and traditions. So consumed were the Jews of Jerusalem by their envies and wrath, that they crucified Jesus in the name of their religion. But He too had a Father, an all wise and all-powerful Father, who delivered Him from their wicked hands. In a show of mighty resurrection power, God raised Jesus from the dead. Then His Father proceeded to establish Jesus as the true and eternal Deliverer of His people — Deliverer from all the powers of the enemy forever.

14

Revival Needs A Man Of Faith And Valor

The continual unfolding of the purposes of God to His chosen servant usually depends upon how he responds to each word given to him. Right attitudes, inward truthfulness, the will to obey, and faith in His word are the elements that God requires to continue to enlarge the revelation of His will and purposes.

Unacceptable responses such as unbelief, rebellion, recriminations, anger, or any other such negative reactions that offend God will cause divine communication to cease. Revelation from God concerning His purposes for a life progresses in a step-by-step manner. The story of Gideon very aptly illustrates this important factor in communing with God.

God began the process of revelation of His true nature and will by sending His heavenly Messenger to Gideon. The Angel opened the conversation with a strange yet brief salutation. The pithy word contained an apparently contradictory truth which invited an answer from Gideon. Then quietly the Angel waited for Gideon's response.

Gideon arose to that challenge by pouring out his heart in burning questions, and thereby, he revealed his secret but true thoughts concerning Jehovah, the evil circumstances of Israel, and the troublings of his own heart. Gideon answered the Angel with protests, confusions, unbelief, and words full of hurt. Illogically enough, this was an acceptable answer to God because it was truth from his limited understanding.

Although his answer revealed his heart's fears, doubts, and recriminations, the Angel accepted this response, nevertheless. God seeks heart truth as a basis upon which to work with man.

The Angel responded to Gideon's answer by reaffirming His first words, then added another and larger word of faith and revelation. His celestial Visitor did not directly answer Gideon's questions or complaints but only enlarged His first salutation.

Each response by Gideon to the further revelation of truth given by the Angel, whether in word or deed, successfully opened the door for God to give him further revelation of His word and will. Gideon's replies to God's word or commands were acceptable to God and permitted the process of revelation to continue.

God did not reveal to Gideon His whole plan and will at once. Mainly because the struggling peasant farmer was far too unprepared in his faith and his knowledge of Jehovah to receive all that God purposed to reveal to him. Furthermore, Gideon's faith was not yet strong enough to fulfill God's plan.

After every word or command God gave, He waited for Gideon's reaction. An acceptable reply would open the way for God to reveal more of His will and plan of deliverance. And each word from God created a larger deposit of faith in his heart. *"So then faith cometh by hearing, and hearing by the word of God" (Romans 10:17).*

At any period along the way Gideon could have frustrated the grace of God in his life by wrong attitudes or a rebellious reaction. Gideon, in his fears, could have flatly refused the commission or could have refused to cut down the idols of Baal at his house. He could have even run away from such fearsome responsibilities like the prophet Jonah. God still would have delivered Israel for their cry had been heard at the throne of grace, but He would have used another man or would have delivered them in another way.

Each time God spoke, He gave Gideon either a word that would build up his faith, an order to obey that would further his development, or words to reveal another portion of His plan and will. Then each time God again would wait until Gideon had obeyed His last command or had received his last revelation in faith. *"For precept must be upon precept, precept upon precept; line upon line, line upon line; here a little, and there a little" (Isaiah 28:10).*

God works with His people one step at a time; the next order is not given until the last one is completed. It is not man who waits on God, but God who patiently waits for man to receive, believe, and obey the last word given. God was ready from the beginning to use Gideon, but Gideon was not yet ready to be used. Therefore, God chose to prepare him through ever advancing revelations or commands.

Step By Step

Gideon's first need was to possess a living faith in Jehovah. This God did by sending His Angel to him. That encounter with the awesome celestial Presence of his Visitor had a profound impact on Gideon. In that Presence his inner heart and thoughts could be sorted out and come into the light of truth. Such heavenly light quickly separated the myths, suppositions, lies, and deceptions from the truth of God that lay buried therein.

Then the light of truth – shining in his heart – caused him to realize his great need to offer unto God a blood sacrifice to restore a right relationship with Jehovah. By the cleansing blood of the sacrifice of the kid (which looked forward in figure to the Cross of Christ), Gideon's sins were forgiven, and he could have further fellowship with God.

After the blood was shed and the sacrifice made, Gideon was thereby prepared to encounter the purifying, empowering baptism of fire of the Holy Spirit. It was there at the rock-altar in the living Presence of God – embodied in the form of a human Visitor – that the visible, tangible fire of God purified his soul. Gideon's offering laid out upon the rock before the fire was kindled, symbolized that the sacrifice of the Lamb of God crucified on the Cross was absolutely necessary before the Pentecostal fire of the Holy Spirit could come.

Following that revelation, Gideon was taken still deeper into the hidden and shadowy valley of his deceitful heart to see the need for the sanctifying power of God to continue working there. In deep heart-searching by the fire of God, he must have encountered the frightening horrors of conviction of his sins within his own heart. For man to truly know the sinfulness of sin, he must drink the bitter draught of righteous condemnation as a sinner before a holy God. Only after that could he receive the glorious revelation of Jehovah's intrinsic nature of mercy and peace through forgiveness of sin and the glorious revelation of Jehovah Shalom – his God, his Savior, his Help, and his Deliverer.

Gideon passed through that dark valley of repentance and the revelation of his own sinfulness without escaping into either bitterness, discouragement, or even self-pity which blames God for one's own evil. Thereby, his faith was sufficiently developed to receive the sanctifying orders for the outward reformation of his own personal life: viz., throw down your own idols and religious system of worship and reestablish public worship to Jehovah.

By his obedience, at the risk of his life and overcoming the dreadful fears involved in his former pagan worship, Gideon proved himself ready to be God's man for revival. Plus, at the same time, he was enjoying his own personal revival.

Gideon increased and fortified his faith and understanding by fulfilling God's orders. He was becoming ever more ready to face the oncoming challenge of the Midianites. God does not intend that the fulfillment of His orders – even though difficult – bring only pain and sorrow, but that it build courage, faith, and character through acceptance and obedience. Thereby His servant becomes prepared for yet greater things.

Terror In Midian

As a result of the news of Gideon's revival of faith, the Midianites gathered together like a swarm of angry bees about a honey-robber. They determined to destroy Gideon, the propagator of the revival. They intended to crush revival in its very earliest stages before it had a chance to spread any further. They wanted to annihilate the very first outbreak of Jehovah's revival along with all those who dared to embrace it – lest it race like a raging forest fire throughout all the strong trees of Israel.

All too well the Midianites knew that if Israel returned to worship Jehovah and cried out to Him for help that He would hear and come to fight for them. They had not the hope of a flea on a dead dog; they would all be overturned as easily as a dead tree falls in a tornado. Therefore, they determined to act immediately before the Israelites had time to fortify their faith in their Jehovah God.

God's Answer

However, Israel's Jehovah had already been at work; He was far ahead of His enemies. He did not need years to bring forth His plan or prepare a vast trained army. God's one man, Gideon, was rapidly advancing in his preparation. Step-by-step God was getting him ready for this hour of glorious deliverance. God already had His answer ready for the arrogant, presumptuous challenge of the Midianites.

"The kings of the earth set themselves, and the rulers take counsel together, against the Lord, and against His Anointed, saying, 'Let us break their bands asunder and cast away their cords from us.' He that sitteth in the heavens shall laugh: the Lord shall hold them in derision" *(Psalms 2:2-4).*

Spirit Of God

Gideon was now cleansed, sanctified and ready to receive the anointing of the Holy Spirit. *". . . the Spirit of the Lord came upon Gideon, and he blew a trumpet; and Abiezer was gathered (was called) after him" (Abiezer in Hebrew means "father of knowledge".) (Judges 6:34).* This enduement of power of the Spirit came upon a blood-washed, fire-purified, surrendered, and obedient servant that God was preparing. Gideon received an impartation of God's Holy Spirit and power from heaven that came upon him like a mantle to cover and gird him for the great battle that lay ahead.

When the Spirit of God came upon Gideon, He brought with Him Abiezer, that is, the spirit of knowledge and wisdom. Immediately, by that gift of knowledge, Gideon was given to know what to do, and he did it in the power of the anointing of the Holy Spirit that had come upon him. Under the power and wisdom of that anointing flowing through him, he picked up a ram's horn trumpet and blew the challenge of war that mightily resounded in both worlds – over the whole land of Israel above and into the regions of raging darkness below. It reached high into the heavens even into the ears of the Almighty. Its faith inspiring notes were carried far and wide by a myriad of messengers both seen and unseen.

God answered the Midianites by sounding forth a challenge, not a retreat – a fair and valid warning to the endangered enemy, not an abject appeal for a peace treaty. The trumpet blast gave a call to arms to all men of faith left in Israel. The song of the trumpet sang: "Behold, our God is with us! Come and join the victory. March straight into the battle for deliverance." At that inspiring trumpet note the smoldering revival fires burst into flaming flames amongst the tall trees of Israel.

15

God With Gideon

A tremendous surge of power and inspiration flowed through Gideon when the anointing of the Holy Spirit came upon him. He felt as if he stood ten feet tall and could easily accomplish anything God ordered. Under that divine influence he realized that he was no longer dependent solely upon his own strength, but God had come to be with him and to fortify him with divine power from on high. The Angel had said, "Jehovah is with thee," and under the anointing of the Holy Spirit, his faith began to realize the powerful significance of those words.

Gideon looked down into the valley of Jezreel (which means *scattering*) and saw the gathering hordes of the Canaanite Baal-followers. Three armies had allied against Israel. Three enemy nations had gathered there with one purpose, i.e., to kill Gideon the son of Joash. Gideon laughed in joyful anticipation of the coming triumph. For by faith, he could already see the scattering of the enemy armies by the help of Jehovah. Under the fresh inspiration of the Holy Spirit's anointing, even that tremendous host of warriors had not the power to frighten him.

Gideon knew the all-powerful Jehovah of Moses (He Who overcame and humiliated mighty Egypt) and Joshua's Conquering Captain of the hosts of the Lord (He who vanquished the powerful kings of Canaan). Gideon greatly rejoiced in anticipated triumph because the glorious Jehovah Shalom was with him.

The Word Of Faith

"Behold, you Jehovah-hating Midianites," Gideon prophesied as the anointing flowed through his spirit, "before Jehovah you shall be as chaff to my fire and as barley to my flail. You shall flee like wild pigeons at my battle cry. I shall uproot you and tear you down like I tore down the idols of Baal with my father's great bullock. I shall trample you as grapes in the winepress and crush you under my feet. Your blood shall flow freely from my trampling.

"By my God I shall set my people free from your vandalizing cruelties. Do not boast over me too quickly, oh uncircumcised Midianites. Behold, Israel shall be well repaid for her servitude to you by the booty we shall collect from your defeated armies. All of your goods shall be riches to my people. Your army rations and sustaining flocks shall fill our empty stomachs for a long time to come. You shall pay a high retribution for your cruel thievery.

"You shall be torn as a lion tears its prey; none will be able to deliver you. My God shall turn your vicious persecution back upon your own heads, for He has promised me the victory by His immutable word.

"What is the matter, mighty Midian? Why did you feel so helpless against your defenseless Hebrew slaves? They have no sword or spear! Why did you feel the need to seek for so much help from other nations in order to destroy us who are already your vassals? Would you make war on your servants who are without riches for booty or make war on defenseless beggars? What frightened you into such a panic?

"What . . . ? Did you hear a rumor of a revival? Have you heard that we are renewing the worship of mighty Jehovah?

Oh, did that set your mocking lips trembling and your blaspheming hearts pounding? It is well that you tremble and panic fills your hearts, for Jehovah Shalom has come to us to bring us into peace.

"Do you honestly think that the huge numbers of your vast army gathered from three nations shall frighten me or overcome mighty Jehovah who is with me? Do you think you bring us into abject submission and hopeless surrender? Do you expect me, to whom has come the I AM PEACE, to plead for peace at the sight of your mighty army without even a battle? Ha, I hold you all in derision! I laugh at your hordes because our mighty Jehovah has returned His favor to us and answered our cries. He is with me, and with Him I shall smite your whole army to the ground in the power of His mighty Name.

"What might or power have you against Jehovah who is on our side and will fight for us? His anointing and power is upon me; His Spirit inspires and covers me. I shall rejoice and leap for joy as a calf free in the meadow for Jehovah Shalom has spoken His immutable word that I shall triumph over you! I shall not die but live; I shall declare His glorious power over all His enemies."

Gideon Blows The Trumpet

In the euphoria and ecstasy of the anointing of the Holy Spirit and with faith burning as a bright flame in his heart, Gideon continued to blow his trumpet in every direction – north, south, east, and west. Up and down with mighty blasts he also sounded out a call to God's hosts everywhere – a call to arise and join him in his victorious fight against their enemies.

That trumpet call, empowered by the breath of God within Gideon, sped out like the stone from David's sling.

Over hill and valley that divine call echoed into every dwelling. The Spirit of God empowered the sound of that trumpet to inspire anyone with faith who heard it. Those that heard its message became willing messengers to carry its call into every cave, hamlet, and town. Not an able bodied man in Israel failed to hear the battle call or understand what it meant.

Far from being an uncertain sound, Gideon's trumpet call declared an unmistakable certainty that revival had come to Israel. Jehovah God had arisen and had sent His Spirit upon a man of faith. The fires of sacrifice to Jehovah were burning once again in Israel. The trumpet called to one and all to arise and fight, for the time of Divine vengeance had come for the Midianites.

Calling Israel To War

"And if ye go to war in your land against the enemy that oppresseth you, then ye shall blow an alarm with the trumpets; and ye shall be remembered before the Lord your God, and ye shall be saved from your enemies" (Numbers 10:9).

Gideon's trumpet call was an irrevocable proclamation of war to every Israelite who heard it. They all knew that specific call, and no one could mistake its meaning. No one would dare blow that war call unless the Spirit of the Lord was upon him. Every able-bodied man that heard it was challenged in his faith and heart – challenged to leave his occupation and join himself to the company of men who came to help the one who blew that trumpet.

Fair Warning

The militant sound also rang loudly and clearly in the ears of the armies encamped in the valley of Jezreel. It was a fair and fearful warning to the allied nations in the army of Midian. Its triumphantly defiant note was a direct challenge to all the warriors gathered for war.

That trumpet call, empowered by the Spirit of Jehovah, clamored loudly in the enemy's ears and generated debilitating fears and serious doubts as to the outcome of their campaign against Israel. Courage began to melt within the heart of warrior after warrior. In no uncertain terms Gideon's war call thundered the message that Israel and the God of Israel had declared war against them. It defiantly said, "From now on, we – the children of Israel – have arisen in faith to throw off the shackles of bondage to Midian. We will no longer tolerate their oppression and cruelties!"

That declaration gave fair and ample warning to the enemy. They had fair opportunity, if they believed at all in the mighty God of Israel, to surrender, to flee for their lives from the wrath of Jehovah and to be thankful for the warning, or else to persist in their unbelief and rebellion, and to make all the futile preparations they desired for defensive or offensive action.

Their dependence in the false god of Baal and in the might of their numbers was futile. Gideon's trumpet call graciously warned his enemies saying: "Surrender, flee, cease from molesting Jehovah's people while there is time, for the God of Israel has come and will take awful vengeance."

The trumpet's message also informed all three of those idolatrous nations that the God of Israel, Almighty Jehovah, was again with His people. Gideon's act of obedience to the Holy Spirit faithfully declared to the enemy that the time of Israel's deliverance had come. The midnight hour of doom for the Midianites had struck in doleful tones; they would be irreparably destroyed.

Calling For Reviving Faith

The penetrating trumpet blast proclaimed firmly and clearly that Gideon believed in the word Jehovah had spoken to him. The voice of the Holy Spirit's anointing that now rested upon Gideon was also calling through his trumpet to all Israel to return to the faith of their fathers and worship their own true God. That ancient and victorious Israeli battle call was unmistakable to every Hebrew ear. The trumpet's call to arms and to battle had sounded time after time as Joshua's armies had marched triumphantly through Canaan conquering and overthrowing kingdom after kingdom, city after city. Yes, that note was well known to the armies of Israel.

The faith-filled trumpet sound also reminded Israel of the gracious promises of their God; it announced His merciful intention to deliver His suffering people. It foretold God's promise of Redemption for His captive children. Its clarion call authoritatively reverberated the note of hope and help; it sang a glad song that the Presence of God was again dwelling with His people.

Calling To Jehovah

The Spirit inspired message of his trumpet not only called every able-bodied man to rise in faith and join Gideon in the battle, but it also winged heavenward, even to the Throne of God. There it reminded God of His promises and claimed His help and intervention in the coming battle of His people – according to His word to Moses.

The ever alert angelic hosts of the Almighty also heard that ordered summons and immediately began to put themselves in battle array. That martial song reverberated throughout the celestial regions announcing earth's expectations of promised reinforcements from Heaven. All Heaven began to sing the same song of joy and gladness for the anticipated victories of revival. "Let us go join them in this glorious moment of deliverance," sang the angel chorus. "Jehovah, their Deliverer, has again been gracious. He has heard His people's cries and has joined Himself to Israel once again. Revival fires are already burning! Revival faith is flowing, for our God revives hope. We can again sing the songs of victory and joy. Israel has turned again to Jehovah, and mighty victory will be given to them."

The Enemy Heard The Call

Later evidence would show that the enemy had heard Gideon's mighty call; they clearly and fearfully understood the trumpet's message. It trumpeted a burning dread into their idol-besotted minds. However, instead of fleeing while there was yet time, in the obstinacy of their hatred, the armies made hasty preparations for war against Gideon's army. Yet every man of that vast army now knew in his heart that he was fighting against the mighty God of Israel. In place of joyful zest for the coming victory and booty, the soldiers – with mortal apprehension – feasted on fright and cried desperately to Baal and their other gods for help. They knew that Israel had returned to faith in Jehovah and revival was in their midst.

A Call To Hope

The voice of the trumpet's call had not only reached the camp of the enemy, it had also reached those who lived in dens, caves, and strongholds. To the poor, the suffering, and the repentant people of God it was a message of faith and hope.

The gaunt and sickly children, the anguished and worried mothers, the starving youths, the hopeless maidens, the frustrated and depressed fathers heard the heartening message of hope. Gideon's trumpet sang to them in joyous notes, "Jehovah, your great Deliverer, has arisen again in Israel. The time of shame and misery has ended! God has heard your repentant cry. Dry your tearful eyes. Put aside your doleful mourning. Put on your gala garments of praise. Sing again . . . yea, sing again, O Israel, the songs of deliverance."

Gladness filled despairing hearts as hopelessness surrendered to hope. Fear fled before the onslaught of faith. In many homes young men's hearts were kindled with zeal; they took up any iron tool available that could be used in battle and set off towards the valley of Jezreel to join Gideon, the faith-filled trumpet-blower, in his march to victory.

A Blast Into Hell

Inspired by the Spirit of God, the terrible trumpet blast roared like a devastating tornado into hell. Satan's minions could not help knowing the prophetic import of the call to arms as that resulted from Gideon's revival. They knew all too well that Gideon's trumpet foretold the coming of another Deliverer. The Beloved Son Himself would come and challenge all the hosts of hell. Furthermore, the prophetic word – written on earth – clearly declared He would fight with them and win the victory. Hell's armies would be again defeated, and their kingdoms shattered beyond recall.

With such a fearful blast of *"faith in God"* echoing in the galleries of the nether world of darkness, there arose an ear splitting howl of rage and impotent wrath from the hosts of Satan. They vowed to win this battle and prove God wrong; they would go forth to inflame and to possess the Midianites with their own rage and fear of defeat. Then the Midianite armies would join the battle with fierce zeal inspired by their intense hatred against Jehovah and His people.

"We will win! We will win! We will win!" they shouted in demonic determination. "The Almighty shall yet know that we are a force to contend with. His fearful, puny peasant farmer, Gideon, shall fall under our attack. He will be putty in our hands – a straw in our fires. This time we shall show no mercy; we will utterly destroy Israel! Not even a child shall escape our wrath," they howled with fierce wrath as they rushed forth to the valley of Jezreel.

16

32,000 Said, "Let's Go"

After Gideon blew the trumpet under the anointing of the Spirit of the Lord, he anxiously watched and waited. He knew no one would respond to the demands of that call to arms unless Jehovah Himself inspired a man's heart to answer. Gideon realized that no one in his right mind would join him in a war so seemingly ridiculous in the light of human reason. If anyone came, he would certainly have to be constrained to join him by the same Spirit of God that had inspired him to blow the trumpet.

However, as the morning progressed an astounding report spread rapidly throughout the land. "Jehovah has revealed Himself to Gideon in a miraculous way," the inspiring news reported. "He has seen a real Angel from Heaven and has talked with Him." As the story was passed from mouth to ear, it certainly did not lose import in the telling. "Gideon has defied old Baal without a trace of resistance from that so-called god. Worship of Jehovah has been reinstalled and the sacrifices on His altars are burning. Revival has come to Gideon and his house," they said. Many a householder erupted in joy when he heard the good news.

One by one the swordless, shieldless, untrained peasants and youths took heart, and came to join Gideon at his camp. Armed with adz and ax, flail and clubs, all manner of farm tools and all else they could find for battle, they came with brawny arms and high spirits. Some came rejoicing in the anticipated booty, some came for curiosity, others for adventure, while others, hesitant and fearful, just came, nevertheless. All day long they came walking over hills, over rocky terrain and through the cropless barren fields that had been destroyed by the Midianites.

"Is That All?"

By the time the evening shadows grew long, all those that responded to the trumpet call gathered together at the well. In astonished alarm Gideon looked at a pitifully small number of men. In his high moment of faith and euphoria he had expected almost every available man in Israel to come. He couldn't believe it at first, so he counted them all again. Yes, there was no doubt, there were thirty-two thousand – no more, not one more. How could such a micro-army fight against the half a million plus trained warriors facing them? They were like a small hare in a meadow with a hungry lion. Gideon's soul was grieved to see how few of his countrymen were willing to fight for liberty and life.

He was tempted to send them all home again and forget all about victory. But the wonderful revelation of Jehovah in his life and mind had fortified his faith; it had taken him beyond the point of turning back. He decided to go ahead and do his best with what Jehovah had given him. After all, he had blown the trumpet; he would be ashamed to quit now. Besides, there were really too many to send them all home ... yet, too few to reasonably face the Midianite hosts.

Gideon faced his dilemma honestly. "How can I ever form an invincible army with so few soldiers?" he pondered. "How is it possible to develop such a rag-tag, undisciplined group of men into a cohesive effective fighting force, especially out of such a small group of men and with such little time to train them before the battle? How will it be possible to get them to function as a real company of fighting men? Will they even accept my orders? Will fear overpower their faith and valor as they face such an immense body of trained warriors? We have very little time I know; after that trumpet call the Midianites will not wait long before attacking us, ready or not."

Only thirty-two thousand young men had faith enough to respond favorably to the trumpet's call. They only had a little reviving of their faith through hearing Gideon's testimony, therefore many barely had sufficient courage to present themselves for battle. "At last," these farmers and would-be-warriors said to themselves, "God has answered our cry; we heard the exciting note of victory in Gideon's trumpet call. In our hearts we feel it must be true what the people are saying. Gideon has actually seen an Angel of God who told him to arise against the Midianites. That is enough for us. We believe his report. No one would dare blow that trumpet call to war into the ears of the Midianites unless he knew Jehovah was with him.

"Did you hear," they asked one another, "that Gideon defiantly tore down the altars of Baal and the gods of the Amorites and not one god dared to touch him? Furthermore, not even a tiny lightning flash came against Gideon from old Baal. We never did feel that Baal was all his priests said he was.

"Nothing but an old cheat, if you ask me," said one. "I also heard that Gideon has reestablished the worship of our former Jehovah God; he has raised an altar on the very rock the Angel set aflame with the fire of God. What more do we need? We will arise and join him in the battle. If Jehovah be with us, we shall surely overcome. Imagine the booty we shall recover from those thieving Midianites. Ha, we will go home rich from this battle."

However, some more fearful than others asked, "But what if we get killed in this battle? What if we do not win? What if we all are slain? After all, everyone thought we would easily win the battle with the Midianites seven years ago, but what a disastrous defeat! Everyone said that Baal, Chemosh, and all the other gods were with us, but not one of them ever showed up to help; they just let us get a terrible beating."

However, others optimistically answered, "But this time is different. Jehovah sent an Angel to Gideon; the Angel told Gideon to fight the Midianites because Jehovah would be with him. Why, even if a few of us are killed, by far the most of us will return greatly enriched. After all, our fathers have all told us that Israel is Jehovah's nation; if He has come to deliver us, then Midian will be defeated. Surely there are tens of thousands of young men who can fight with us. We shall join Gideon, fight the battle, and become rich and famous as valiant warriors. Our neighbors, friends, and families will be proud of us; we will be very popular."

Where Were The Rest?

However, sad to relate, there were many thousands of Israeli young men who heard the trumpet call, understood what it meant, but in their fear and unbelief stayed home. In their cowardice and lack of faith they refused to respond to the divine call to battle. Their courage was battered and destroyed by their miserable state of servitude. Their unbelief in Jehovah was highly magnified by the deception of the Amorite demon-gods. Therefore, the better thoughts of zeal, obedience, and valor were completely negated by their doubts and fears.

They said to themselves, "It is useless, we haven't a chance for victory. Why join those zealots and die the death of a deluded martyr? How do we know Gideon is not some self-deceived fanatic that thinks he saw an angel? If he wants to commit suicide that way, let him go, but that is no reason we should follow him into death.

"After all, who is Gideon? Who ever heard of him before now? What has he done to prove his prowess and military skills that we should trust and follow him? Warfare is not a game; if we lose, we die. We are too young to die. He is not a warrior, a nobleman, nor a rich man. He possesses no name of importance in Israel. Why then should we run after him just because he blows a trumpet?

"Alright, . . . maybe he does mean well; of course, we all would like to see an end to this miserable occupation and Midianite rule – but fight their whole army without having one proper weapon for war? He must be out of his right mind!

"Also, when we come to think of it, it would absolutely be suicide for us to even be seen with Gideon. Everyone who joins him will be marked as a traitor and a rebel. No thank you! We will stay quietly at home. And . . . if he wins, we will enjoy the victory without taking those terrible deadly risks."

Darkest Before Dawn

Thirty-two thousand and no more! What a testimony to the spiritual decadence in backsliding Israel. Of all the tens of thousands of young men of battle age, only thirty-two thousand joined Gideon at the well of Harod – the well of trembling. How shameful that faith could only be found in such a small number of young men in Jehovah's Israel! The misery of their captivity and the deception of their idolatry had saturated their souls with fear of Baal and unbelief in their own God.

The parents of these young men had long before turned away from Jehovah to serve Baal. Therefore, their children had not been taught to know or to believe in Jehovah. The spiritual fall of the nation had begun in their homes. The young prosperous parents enjoyed the prosperity of God's blessing on their fields and lives. They left the faith of their fathers and turned to enjoy the sensual tempting fertility rites of the Amorite gods. The worship of Jehovah was a thing of the past generation. That old religion was definitely worn out and definitely not modern.

Truly, it was a pitifully small number of untrained peasant soldiers that came to face the multitudinous well-armed hosts of the Midianites. Even so, it was a wonder that thirty-two thousand young men were willing to march off to war. It was more for the desire for riches and booty and to break out of their misery than it was to renew any worship of Jehovah. Revival had not yet reached the hearts of most of them.

The hands of these young men were weaponless. Apart from the help of Jehovah, these raw recruits posed no serious threat to the Midianites. Were it not so dangerous, such a ludicrous undertaking would be laughable – except for one thing – Jehovah was with them.

Decision Time

The battle call of the trumpet demanded a decision. It was not a selective summons to just a few; it called to every able-bodied man in Israel. Everyone knew what the trumpet's message meant. Not one could honestly say, "I haven't been called to the army of the Lord." The call to serve Jehovah and present one's self as a volunteer for the battle of the Lord was not for a chosen few, but was an unlimited call to all.

Everyone who heard the call of the trumpet was morally and spiritually obligated to volunteer. Each one had to choose either to stay home in fear and unbelief (and enjoy the benefits gained by others, if any) or to join the warriors and risk death for the deliverance of each's wife, children, home, and land.

Those who heard the trumpet call and yet remained behind cringing in their office-caves, school-dens, or economic strongholds were a shame to their nation and to their God. They would have no part in the distribution of the spoils of battle, nor have their names written in the roster of faithful soldiers of Jehovah's army. Those would be forever marked as too fearful and unbelieving to present themselves for the battle of the Lord.

The Hosts Of Midian

When the thirty-two thousand newly arrived volunteers peeped over the edge of the hill into the valley of Jezreel, they saw an immense expanse of the Midianite army camped below them. They recoiled in shocked dismay. Suddenly they were frightened into reality; they took stock of their situation and realized how few and weaponless they were. Seeing the force and might of the enemy camp, many of those young peasants completely lost their dreams of riches and glory. They had little confidence in the Almighty Jehovah that Gideon said was with them. Many of their hearts melted within them; their courage was wiped out by the paralyzing fear which was engendered by their unbelief.

Faced with the humanly impossible task of delivering his people from the Midianites with such a small, unprepared, and weaponless army, Gideon also began to wonder. Had he somehow made a mistake? Had he missed some divine order? Had he failed to hear God's voice? Had he erred in understanding what God had said to him? Gideon knew Jehovah Shalom was real and had spoken to him. So with his new faith under attack, he turned to his God for the answers.

17

Gideon's Faith Tried

What irrational military odds! A paltry thirty-two thousand farmers pitted against approximately half a million armed warriors with only a couple of days for preparation before the battle forced Gideon to seek special help from Jehovah Shalom, "IF THOU WILL SAVE ISRAEL BY MY HAND..." Then he stopped and thought to himself, "wait a minute, how can there be an *if*? God told me that He would save Israel by my hand.

"But... is it possible that I am mistaken in my timing? Or is there a direction from God I failed to hear? So far, He has not given me any directions as to how to order the battle. Am I somehow erring in the way I am gathering an army? Is that why there are so few? I know the Spirit of God constrained me to blow the call to war on the trumpet. However, did I somehow incorrectly interpret what God meant when He said that our deliverance from the Midianites should be by my hand? He spoke so briefly; perhaps I did not really understand His word or do what He intended.

"Look at my grand army!" he grimaced. "A pitifully small band of untrained men have joined me – all of thirty-two thousand. Am I only deceiving myself and striving under some kind of self-deception? Is it possible that I psyched myself up into some big ego trip? Am I unwittingly trying to make some big name for myself? This is war; it is life or death for us all. I dare not be mistaken; I must be absolutely certain before I take these men into battle.

"One thing is certain, once we join battle there is no turning back. It would be impossible to run and escape from that great horde of heathen warriors who implacably hate us. They would run us all to earth like a great pack of wolves pursuing hinds in the field for sport. I am ready to die for my belief, but is it right to lead this little flock of farmers into the slavering jaws of this murderous army of wrathful Midianites?

"Jehovah Shalom!" he ardently cried out as doubts assailed his mind, "I want to do, . . . yes, and *will do* Your will. I truly believe that I understood You to say that You would deliver Israel from the Midianites through me. That day when the power of Your Spirit came upon me, I felt so certain that I blew the trumpet calling Israel to war.

"Behold, O Lord, our enemies are mighty – an army of trained and well-armed warriors – everyone is thirsting like a tiger for our blood. Only these few thousand unarmed, undisciplined farmers answered the call of the trumpet. While they are full of good intentions, they definitely are not trained soldiers. We are such a small troop! None of us knows anything about warfare for we have never practiced or drilled as an army.

"Give Me A Sign"

"Hear me, O Lord, be not displeased with me, but grant me a sign from Heaven to confirm that I am doing what You want me to do. Prove to me that I am truly in obedience to You and not mistaken; show me that this battle is unmistakably called according to Your orders; confirm that these few thousand men are all the army You need. I pray Thee, let this fleece of wool I lay here in the open field be soaking wet in the early morning and all the earth around it be absolutely dry and dewless."

God knew that His servant Gideon was not seeking to evade obedience or escape from the commanded task. But He also knew that His servant truly needed reassurance in the face of the outward appearance of such enormous odds. Gideon had just a few thousand trembling, untrained peasants with farm tools as weapons; yet mustered in the invisible world were the mighty, invincible hosts of the Almighty waiting totally unseen. Meanwhile the visible antagonists were well armed, experienced warriors – the united armies of three nations. This was enough to make the stoutest heart hesitate.

God did not rebuke Gideon for his request of a sign for confirmation, nor did He show any displeasure at his prayer. God intended Gideon to be fully assured in his faith and therefore was willing and ready to grant this request and give him yet another witness of His spoken word. God wanted His chosen leader to know of a surety that He was truly with him, to know that the battle was the Lord's, and to know he was correctly following orders.

Gideon was not to be left alone in this battle that now raged against his faith. The God of Peace, who is full of mercy and knows man's frame of dust, would not cast His harassed servant aside when he needed the added help of still more assurance. So Jehovah Shalom encouraged His obedient servant's faith by giving him a miraculous sign; while at the same time, He manifested to Gideon His supreme sovereign power over the mighty forces of nature. Those elemental forces of nature had never surrendered the control of their essential elements to the pleas of man.

The following morning Gideon arose to find his fleece so saturated with the dew of the night that he wrung out of it a bowl full of water. And to his amazement and joyful gratitude, all the earth around the wool was as dry as the desert sand; not a drop of dew glistened on a single leaf or blade of grass. All was dry! The dust of the ground remained undisturbed by any moisture from the night dew. God had answered his prayer – the sign was abundantly positive.

Doubts Still Assail

The day wore on and – though Gideon eagerly watched the paths that led to Harod's well – not one more volunteer showed up for his army. Furthermore, no sword, spear, or shield appeared from some hidden cache that a friendly neighbor might have concealed clandestinely. Not even one friendly supportive Israelite brought victuals for his lean and hungry men to help them. The fear of reprisals, if they lost the battle, made every Hebrew family afraid to even offer help to Gideon.

As morning gave away to afternoon and the day waned to a close, the refreshing assurance of the wet fleece on the dry ground slowly faded away as Gideon faced the pragmatic pressure of the very real and contrary circumstances that faced him. Suddenly the upsetting thought came to him, "Could it be possible that someone inadvertently found and used my fleece during the night?" Niggling doubts began to assail his mind, "Someone might have unintentionally tampered with my fleece and left no sign of footprints in the hard dry ground." The heavy responsibility of the lives of his fellow Israelites would not let him rest in peace.

Gideon again began to question his own audacity and to analyze his ridiculous endeavor. No more help of any kind or nature came to the little army of desperate men. According to their natural resources there was no way for them to win the victory. Outside of a mighty miracle, they were walking straight into mortal catastrophe.

God had not spoken another word to Gideon, nor had He indicated in what way He would bring forth the victory. He had provided the men with neither sword nor shield; nor had He even told them what weapons He would use or where they would come from.

Meanwhile, all the weapons they possessed were the few unsharpened farm tools they had brought with them for arms. A few foresighted men managed to bring a bit of meal with them from their scant supply, but many did not even have that recourse. They had to fill their hungry bodies as best they could with nothing more than water from Harod's well.

Hour by hour Gideon's assurance wilted. As he pondered his options and analyzed his position, logic and prudence made Gideon consider that after all he could be terribly, tragically wrong. "This is not just a practice session," he reflected, "this is either life by an absolute miracle or sure death by my foolish suicidal action. I am venturing the lives of this band of volunteers – the lives of many villagers and my own life in this battle. If I am mistaken . . .

"Oh, what a dreadful responsibility! If I am wrong, I will take to the grave with me the guilt of all these lives; I cannot bear the thought of being the one who leads my fellow Israelites into the grave. I must be more than sure that I am right; I must be positive God is with me. We are in need of a miracle and nothing less."

Gideon Prayed Again

Again Gideon – in humility, with deep heart searching and the fear of the Lord upon his soul – directed his prayer to his God of Peace. With deep heart wrenching groans he cried, "O Jehovah Shalom, do not be angry with me! I want to please You and not falter in unbelief, but I am so concerned about the welfare of all these people. Only you, Jehovah Shalom, can help us by Your Almighty power.

"I feel what I am doing is right and in obedience to your will, but I am only human and can be so wrong. I have no one else to turn to – no one but You to counsel with. I dare not counsel with these men as to battle plans or weapon strategy lest I tear down their already small faith.

"God of Israel, in your mercies do me this favor – in the morning let this fleece be as dry as the dust of the wilderness and all the earth around it remain saturated with dew. Once again let the inviolate laws of nature be broken in such a way that no human intervention can possibly hinder such a miracle. God of miracles, confirm my way once more beyond all doubt I humbly plead. Before You give us the triumphant miracle of deliverance, confirm my way by this miracle."

Again he found his Jehovah Shalom merciful and understanding of his hurting heart. God was quite willing to reassure Gideon in his difficult pathway of faith in blind obedience – a way that led into the dead end of absolute foolishness when judged by any kind of human evaluation.

At His Word

That night the Creator of all worlds gave special orders concerning the laws of nature. To the dew of the night Jehovah ordered that it condense abundantly all the night long and soak the land as if it had rained copiously upon the dry ground. "But there is one place," He commanded, "you must not fall. Near the well of Harod there is a fleece of wool laying on the ground; you must pass it by with not one single drop condensing upon it." And He dispatched a mighty angel to stand guard and to watch all night lest a single drop of dew mistakenly condense upon that fleece.

Also, God spoke to the winds and told them to blow with their driest breath exclusively and only upon that fleece of Gideon. He told them to blow upon it until any moisture it may have resident within it had been fully drawn out by morning. "It must be as dry as the dust of the Negev," He commanded them. And the winds and the dew obeyed His voice.

And so it was that in the morning, as the first rays of dawn broke over the Israeli hills, Gideon anxiously went to his fleece. As he walked through the grass, it was wet as if there had been rain all the night long. In the presence of such abundant moisture soaking his sandals, Gideon's heart filled with trepidation as he approached the fleece.

Lo, It Was Very Dry

When Gideon drew near to the fleece, he specifically noted there was not a single foot track marring the dew around that fleece; no one had been there to interfere with his sign. With his heart pounding in apprehension, he picked up his fleece, and lo, it was very dry. When Gideon's hands touched its thirsty arid fibers – in the midst of abundant moisture – a flame of faith ignited in his heart burning out every fear, every doubt, and every concern that had found lodging there.

Gideon's faith suddenly crystallized into a new certainty in his heart. Somehow this last miracle, showing such sovereign power over the inviolate laws of nature, inspired his faith to anchor itself firmly in the confirmed word of God.

Jehovah had answered his prayers in such a way that it was impossible to doubt. This miracle could not possibly be some accident of nature; this was an impossible achievement for the blind laws of nature to execute. This could only be done by the Creator Himself who held all power over nature in His hand. He who commanded the forces of nature in the plagues of Egypt and piled on high the waters of the Red Sea – the very God of Moses – had answered Gideon's prayer.

"If Jehovah can work such impossibilities and order the laws of nature to do His bidding for me," Gideon's glad mind reasoned, "then that same God can just as easily work another impossibility and give us glorious victory over all the Midianites.

"It is true, true, true!" he cried out exulting in faith. "I am called of God. The word the Angel gave to me at Old Solitary is as true as Jehovah Himself. Jehovah Shalom never lies; He is my peace! I have not misinterpreted His word." And so Gideon marched back to his tent with the steps of a conqueror.

18

Gideon's Army?

Gideon's spirit was immeasurably encouraged by the compassionate grace and sovereign authority manifested in the answer to his request for a sign of confirmation. Gideon knew he had asked for an extraordinary miracle to be manifested before his eyes as a sign that this enterprise was truly being done in obedience to Jehovah's command. And God, tenderly understanding the very human weakness of his peasant-servant, graciously granted his prayer.

If perchance some rare quirk of nature or man-made interference had made the first trial of his fleece accidental, not so the second – that dry fleece could not possibly be accidental nor coincidental. That dust-dry fleece in the midst of all that water was absolute and conclusive evidence of a miraculous intervention by Jehovah. Jubilant Gideon serenely marched towards his little army in the full assurance of faith that flooded his soul.

The God of Peace had heard and answered his prayers; Gideon had put his trust in Him. It was the very God who worked such a phenomenal miracle in the realms of the inviolate laws of nature who was leading him in this wondrous venture. Gideon was no longer a victim of doubts. It was true; it was certain – Jehovah Shalom, the God of Abraham, Moses, and Joshua was with him. The living God listened to his prayers and answered his requests; Jehovah and Gideon were communicating. All was well!

In the strength of his reconfirmed faith, Gideon put aside worrying; Jehovah was supporting him in a tangible, down-to-earth way. In this assurance, he was now ready to press ahead. His God would supply the needed miracles of weapons and all the tactical direction to win the victory. Despite any or all adverse situations that might arise, he was ready to trust God. Had not God answered his prayers, proving beyond doubt his miraculous powers?

However, little did Gideon realize how much he would need that assurance. Shortly thereafter, his faith would face an even greater test. But for the moment, it was sufficient that God had confirmed His command. Once again, it was Gideon's turn to respond to God's command.

Following the early morning miracle of the saturated fleece, Gideon proceeded to gather his army together and make preparations to go up against the enemy encamped in the shadows of the valley below.

The Infection Of Fear

Gideon and his men, as a flock of helpless sheep, had bivouacked on the sides of Mt. Gilead near the well called Harod, which means *trembling*. From there they could look down into the valley of Jezreel upon the encampment of the Midianite army. As his small army gazed down into the valley – filled with the uncountable hordes of armed soldiers ready to attack – many of Gideon's followers began to tremble in mortal fear.

Insidiously contagious fear spread from one to another faster than a plague and was more virulent than a deadly fever. It was impossible for those farmers-turned-soldiers not to see the ludicrously unequal odds of the dreadful challenge before them. It was impossible for them to overcome their fear of walking into that incongruous conflict. One would-be-soldier after another became infected and seriously ill with the crippling infirmity of mortal terror. At the sight of that huge army below, their small faithless courage wilted, expiring as easily as a fish tossed upon the sandy shore. All of their good intentions were demolished as they became mesmerized by the mighty Midianite army with their powerful conventional weapons of war.

Because God had determined to use powerful weapons that demanded fearless faith to wield, He could not use frightened fighters in His army. God did not intend to use the normal weapons of sword, spear, and shield; instead, He had chosen weapons that demanded obedient trust and anointed courage to wield in battle. Therefore, fear-filled farmers could not fight effectively with His choice of powerful, but unconventional weapons.

The first invincible weapon God had determined to use was the piercing voice of the triumphant trumpet. Fainthearted farmers, with their good intentions tragically undermined by fear-generated unbelief, would not have the courage to stand in the very face of the enemy and blow a mighty trumpet blast with all their might.

God Rejects The Fearful

As Gideon was looking over his gathered army, God spoke to him. It was a most amazing word – to all natural thinking it was completely irrational. The Voice that Gideon had learned to know and trust said, "Gideon, the people who are with you are too many."

"Too many?" blurted out Gideon in the sudden shock. "Am I hearing right?" he queried himself in complete surprise. "God," Gideon answered the Voice he was hearing, "I have fretted for two days because there are so pitifully few. It is such a small army and so pathetic to behold in the face of such odds. I have wondered much if I was really rightly obeying Your instructions."

"Gideon," the Voice continued, "they are too many. Many of the men are with you, but they are not with Me. All of those who volunteered are not the ones I have chosen. They are too many for Me to use. Not all of them are ready for My army. Many are sick at heart, trembling with fright and utterly debilitated with fear and unbelief. Their fears would cause them to turn back in the heat of battle. It will be much better without them.

"If I use all these men to win the battle, they would vaunt themselves against Me and say that it was by their own might and valor that they won the battle. Then Israel would not admit that it was I who gave them the victory, and they would not return to Me. They would continue worshiping and construe the victory to their idols. I can only use men of courage and valor, Gideon, your army is too large for Me to use."

God had carefully prepared Gideon; He had put His divine faith in His servant's heart, had turned him away from his idolatry, and had brought him to yield in obedience to His will. However, most of these volunteer farmers, not as yet having begun to worship Jehovah, would not give Him the glory but would only praise themselves. They would think their own valor and expertise in war had won the battle. They would also claim that their false gods had helped them, thus giving the honor to their idols. Thereby, they would completely disregard the intervention of Jehovah; they would thwart the very purpose of God's intervention.

These peasant-serfs knew nothing of the cleansing blood of sacrifice unto Jehovah which would lead them to the yet-hidden Cross and the purifying fire that God had shown Gideon. Most of them would ridicule the necessity of throwing down their Baal and of destroying their own groves in order to return to Jehovah, the true God of Israel.

Spiritually, they were conspicuously unprepared. They were helpless due to their fears and shackled by their unbelief. They could only be sorted out and sent home. In His infinite wisdom God knew that those who still worshiped their idols at home could not have the faith in Jehovah to stand fearlessly in battle against such a fortified enemy.

"Gideon," God continued, "tell all the people who are fearful and terrified – those even now trembling with fear – to leave Mount Gilead and return home. Tell them that they will not be needed in this battle. They may go back home to their loved ones and await the victory in safety. They may go tonight in the darkness, thereby they will not be ashamed to be seen escaping the conflict. Furthermore, Gideon, they will not resent this order; the fearful will be very glad for the opportunity to slip away in the dark. Each one will think that they are the only one – that no one will miss them. Because there has been no roll call and their names are not listed, they may leave without chagrin before their fellow farmers."

That order did not sound too extreme a proposition to the naive ears of Gideon. In the strength of his own renewed faith, he expected that only a few of his brave souls would be missing in the morning. Really, a few dozen at the most would admit their fearfulness and slip out during the night and with such a small army already, a few more or less would make no real difference. He slept soundly that night assured that all was well.

Empty Ranks

When the rays of the morning sun awakened the camp, Gideon called his troops to order. Troops . . . ? What troops . . . ? Where were they? He could not believe his eyes. The unbelievable reduction in the size of his army shocked him. The light of day revealed that a massive exodus had taken place while darkness had reigned during the night. Massive gaps of empty space riddled the ranks; most of his army had escaped homeward like frightened rabbits hearing a baying hound.

They had seen the enormous three-nation army of the Midianites stretched out for leagues in the valley and compared it with their own small numbers. They had also realized that not one of them had a sword or a shield for weapons; their self-appointed commander had no store or cache of standard armor or swords – nor any other normal weapon.

Those who left had said to themselves, "This whole scheme of battle is suicidal! We have no chance of winning this battle. We will be slaughtered like sheep penned up with lions. Gideon has gone mad; his vision is false for it cannot be true. His testimony of meeting an Angel of God was nothing more than a hallucination. Who else, besides Gideon, saw the Angel or heard Him declare that Jehovah is with us? None of our priests have had any angelic visitation to confirm Gideon's tale. Let's get out of here before the enemy sees us, identifies us, and kills us for insurgency and rebellion.

"We want to be delivered from the turmoil and strife of the Midianites as much as anyone else, but not at the suicidal price this battle will cost. As to revival, certainly we want revival! It would be nice to have the old worship of Jehovah renewed in our land, but is it worth the price of having to tear down all our previous forms, practices, and images of worship like Gideon did? And if we did, what would our friends and neighbors say? At best, the Baal worshipers would be furious and call us the Gideonite Cult of Jehovah Worshipers; at worst, they would despise us, mock us, and try to kill us.

"Furthermore, even if in the heat of the battle we somehow escaped with our lives, what would our friends and neighbors say of us? People like winners and despise losers! We will surely be defeated and be the losers. It's as easy to see as that mob of Midianites in Jezreel's plains – it's impossible for us to win this battle. Our neighbors will laugh us out of our land. We will be ridiculed forever as fools who went out like a flock of silly chickens to fight a pack of foxes and quite naturally lost the battle.

Weighed And Found Wanting

The overshadowing Presence of God sifted out the hearts of men that night; over two-thirds of Gideon's volunteers surrendered to their fears. Their actions confessed their unbending, rebellious unbelief in Jehovah, the God of Israel. Twenty-two thousand frightened fighters abandoned Gideon and his cause of deliverance; shamelessly they stole out of the camp. By rationalizing arguments, they appeased their consciences and returned home, leaving the field to the more courageous few.

Fear of the enemy and worship of false gods left a very small faith with which to wage war. The fear of the enemy's swords, fear of the gods of the land, fear of the gods of the enemy, and fear for their lives ruled their thoughts. Their unbelief in Jehovah – that was most offensive in the eyes of the Lord – made them useless in the battle of deliverance. Nevertheless, Jehovah loved them and would proceed to deliver them and turn them back to Himself.

Because of their fear, they could not fit into God's chosen means of victory. God could not use them in His tactics for this war. Having such a debilitating weakness, they had to be sent home, defeated even before the battle had begun – self-defeated by their own unbelief, fears, and idolatries.

That morning Gideon found himself left with an army of only ten thousand – immensely less than the size of the army he had considered necessary. However, God had prepared His chosen man for this shattering decrease by answering his two fleeces, thereby confirming his faith. Gideon did not doubt that God's Presence was with him and that his Jehovah Shalom, who thoroughly controlled the elements of nature, would bring a devastating defeat to the enemy. Gideon remained strong in his faith, obeying, and believing that his Jehovah Shalom Lord was with him.

19

God Chooses His Men

Before He inspired Gideon to sound the trumpet call to war, God had brought Gideon through the trial of his faith by obedience. Now He would bring the men whom He would use in His battle into the trial of their faith also. Those who would bring Israel into revival and renewed faith must first have a strong faith themselves and a total commitment working in their own hearts. Faith is far more imperative in the forefront of battle than before the actual battle is joined. All the men who would enter into God's battle must have their faith tried and established, even as their leader Gideon.

God had already weighed the fearful, unbelieving, and idolatrous volunteers in His balance. He had found them wanting and sent them home. Now God would lead the ten thousand who remained into an astute ingenious trial that would clearly determine the men whose faith and courage would measure up to God's prerequisites.

God did not permit Gideon to judge the men in this deeper soul-sifting trial. Infinite Wisdom Himself would be the One to prove and select which ones would be suitable to be in His army. This selection would not rest upon character analysis or outward appearance, but upon God's thorough scrutiny of the hearts of those men.

It was the same divine principle that God followed many years later, when he chose David as the next king from the sons of Jesse. "... *the Lord said unto Samuel, 'Look not on his countenance, or on the height of his stature; because I have refused him: for the Lord seeth not as man seeth; for man looketh on the outward appearance, but the Lord looketh on the heart'"* (1 Samuel 16:7).

Yet Too Many?

Gideon was again caught by surprise when God spoke to him concerning his army, "... *The people are yet too many; bring them down unto the water, and I will try them for thee there: and it shall be, that of whom I say unto thee, 'This shall go with thee,' the same shall go with thee; and of whomsoever I say unto thee, 'This shall not go with thee,' the same shall not go"* (Judges 7:4).

"Too many . . . ? Ten thousand are too many . . . ? Am I losing my senses? Am I hearing voices like someone who is deluded or even demented?" Gideon wondered. "Am I so mixed up under these pressures that I have lost the ability to distinguish God's voice? How could God possibly say such an unrealistic, absurd thing when this motley company is already over two-thirds reduced? Too many . . . ? No, it just could not possibly be . . . and yet. . . .

". . . And yet, God, I know it was Your Voice; I cannot mistake it. As a mother recognizes the voice of her babe, I recognized it as surely. I cannot pretend or say it was not Your Voice, for there is no other voice like Yours in all the world. When You speak to me, Your Voice surges through my whole being as a holy fire. It impinges Itself indelibly upon my spirit.

"I honestly confess that I don't understand Your ways, but I know what You have told me to do. After all, this is Your battle . . . not mine, so I will obey You and do what You have said. I am fully persuaded that You shall win this battle whether with many or with few."

Gideon's company had no warning from God or Gideon that they would be tried and judged by their own natural responses to a given situation. They had no awareness that the inner attitudes – those which governed their outer actions – would indisputably mark them and become the criteria of their position in God's plan.

When they least expected it and were quite oblivious to all that was entailed in their actions, God would examine, judge, and choose certain ones from among all the rest. The place and the manner that God determined to use for this examination was simple, casual and yet most unique.

To The Waters Of Judgment

God commanded Gideon, "Bring them down unto the water, and I will try them for thee there." Flowing water typifies the moving of the Spirit of God in times of revival. A flowing stream of water also signifies the stream of living water that flows from the Throne of God.

Through this symbolic action God was saying, "I will cause the stream of My life and gracious blessings to flow before them, and I will scrutinize each man's motives and reactions as they drink of My stream. Their own individual and natural response to My waters will define their place in My army of overcomers.

In obedience to God's command, Gideon led the remaining ten thousand men to the waters to quench their thirst and fortify themselves for the battle. Their commander wondered greatly what their responses and their attitudes would be. He knew that their actions, the result of their heart attitudes, would be the basis of God's selection; their actions would divide them into two companies – those accepted and chosen by God, and those who would be rejected and counted as unfit for the battle for revival.

Wise Warriors

Carefully and cautiously – well aware that at any moment the enemy could launch a surprise attack upon them – certain men lifted the water to their mouths in their cupped hand and sipped it. Such a soldier was alert and vigilant; his mind and heart were thoroughly attuned to the coming battle. He was too concerned and conscious of the danger of the enemy army at hand to foolishly put himself off guard while basking and reveling in the delicious delight of the refreshing stream on that hot day.

Those were the ones who were ever mindful of the proximity of the enemy who even now might be in hiding – waiting like lions in ambush. Such men were not ones to be caught unawares – flat on the ground with their faces in the water. The enemy would not catch them satiating themselves on the sweet blessings of the cool waters and totally unprepared for battle.

To them the refreshing of the water was a means to an end, the refreshing they needed to enable them to fight the enemy. The deliverance of God's people from captivity was far more important in their minds than surrendering to the delightful pleasure of the cool waters on that hot afternoon. Such men would not allow self-gratification to rob them of their caution, expose themselves to a surprise assault and bring defeat before they even started to fight. Such foolishness was unthinkable! They would not waste this God given opportunity of bringing deliverance to God's people.

Such alert, valiant ones were not only aware of the coming battle but were eagerly and courageously looking forward to it. They believed in Jehovah and their faith firmly assured that the battle would be won. They determined not to lose sight of the preeminent purpose of fighting for deliverance by surrendering themselves to the refreshing delights of the waters from the cool, crystal stream. As delightful as the waters were, these were men with a divine appointment; the divine purpose reigned supreme in their hearts. One by one, as each sipped the water from his hand, unknowingly he set himself apart as chosen and appointed by God to form His troop of warriors.

One by one, Gideon counted them as God pointed them out to him. The hand-drinkers he sent over into a company by themselves . . . one here . . . one there . . . and yet another over there. "O God, how few they are!" he thought. When it was all over, Gideon could count only three hundred men in the company which God had determined as His army. Even though he counted them over several times to make sure, there were three hundred – no more, not one more, that was all. That was the number of Gideon's army as commissioned by Jehovah. A very little band – but a band who believed in a very big God.

The Cost Of Self-Enjoyment

The rest of the men thought the battle of lesser importance than enjoying the benefits of the cool stream. Their attitude was, "Get all you can when you can and enjoy it. Live for today for tomorrow we may die. Be sure and get all the blessing and refreshing you can."

Deliverance of their families and nation was of less importance than personal self-gratification. They sought the invigorating blessings of the stream as an end in itself. Their self-seeking spirit ignored or forgot the danger in which they had thereby placed themselves. They were too self-centered and self-minded for the eminent danger to enter their minds.

They unwisely surrendered themselves to the joy of the moment – thoughtless of the wiles and danger of the unseen enemy.

They participated in that moment of blessing and refreshment for their own enjoyment. They did not realize that they must be ever watchful – that the use of the refreshing waters was only to strengthen them for the battle of deliverance of God's groaning captives. These men were the selfish ones to whom personal joy, blessing, and refreshment were more important than fighting God's enemies for the deliverance of His people.

True, they did not fear the Midianites; they were brave, but their bravery was untried bravado and was based on the naivete of inexperience. They did not suspect how cunning, deceitful, and deadly their enemies could be. They were not whole-heartedly committed to God for the deliverance of Israel.

These – who wanted to be God's warriors – lay on their bellies with their face in the cool waters; they formed the second company. This company God judged unfit to have a part in His battle. Nine thousand seven hundred men were separated and placed into that company; nine thousand seven hundred found themselves rejected by Jehovah. Gideon counted them several times to be sure. Then with keen sorrow in his heart, Gideon sent them away from the battle to find their own place at home and to await the outcome of that climactic encounter ahead.

The rejected ones typify those who seek the blessings of God; those who come to the place where the streams of God's grace are flowing and yet who seek those waters mainly for their personal benefit and advantage. They are more interested in using that refreshing stream for blessing and enjoyment than they are to be enabled to overcome and find deliverance from their enemies.

Midianites represent a type of worldly Christian who follows the idolatries of the world and bring strife and confusion into the Church. The tribes of Amalek, a son of Esau, are a type of carnal-minded churchgoers who profess religion but worship idols in their hearts. And Ishmael depicts a type of mixture of world philosophies and the religion of Jehovah. These three nations that rose up against Israel are ever the enemies of the true followers and disciples of Jesus; they will seek to mislead the true believers into their own worldly ways whenever possible. They hate revival with a pure hatred. They will seek to stop, hinder, and quench a revival move with all means and weapons at their disposal. When such ones inhabit the coasts of Israel, they will always try to quench all fires of devotion and faith; they seek to bring the cold breath of death and the hurting pains of spiritual apathy into the people.

When revival streams of refreshing begin to flow, they will always separate the true Church of God into three camps: those who will become the overcomers and do exploits for Christ, those who will be blessed and enjoy the refreshing but will never enter into the company of those who will follow the Lamb whithersoever He goeth, and those who will flee completely away in fear to await the outcome of the revival and then see if they can enter and receive.

Special Weapons Are For Special Men

Self-gratifying blessing-seekers could not qualify for God's army. One reason was that the weapons God had chosen to fight this battle would not have been acceptable to them. Self-centered men could not bring themselves to blow the trumpet and break a pitcher that would release the blazing fire of their torches in their own faces in plain sight of the enemy.

They would not have enough faith to announce their whereabouts and illuminate themselves, and by that action become the obvious target of every spear and arrow in the Midianite arsenal. Due to their small faith and devotion, they would panic and flee in terror from the enemy; they would cause their companions to flee also. Such self-pleasing ones could not bear to find themselves in the light of their own torch facing the enemy's swords in the dark of the night.

The pitcher that was broken typifies the denial of self which Jesus demanded for His disciples. When Mary broke her alabaster box of ointment, she . . . by so doing . . . demonstrated her surrendered, poured out, and committed life unto God. In like manner, God's chosen men must also be broken vessels that are surrendered and committed to the Master's will.

The rejected men had not this level of commitment; they could not stand in the dark hour of battle against the enemy's raging. They blithely carried over the dominating spirit of self-love into the things of God, and in doing so they disqualified themselves from the real battle. Though the nine thousand seven hundred had passed the first test of courage and had overcome their fears generated by beholding the hosts of the enemy, nevertheless, they were far too self-centered to stand fearless in the heat of swordless, shieldless battle. Seeking their own glory and blessing, these men looked forward more to booty than deliverance. God also knew that – if He brought such self-seeking, pleasure-seeking men into victory – they would undoubtedly seek to bring praise to themselves rather than give the glory to God. Such ones God could not use in the great decisive battle that lay ahead. They were too full of self-worship to bring a revival of Jehovah-worship to Israel.

The Real Warriors Are Found

After being judged at the waters, there were only three hundred fighters left. Ninety-seven percent were judged unworthy of being participants in this victorious company; what a tragic percentage of unfit ones! Whether too fearful, too unbelieving, too self-loving, or too unconcerned, they were judged and rejected by God as participants in His army.

However, though God rejected them as warriors, nevertheless, they too would receive the precious benefits of Israel's deliverance. They too would be able to enjoy the fruits of the revival. But in the rich rewards of victory, they would not participate.

After this extensive pruning of Gideon's army, the God-of-All-Comfort spoke sweet words to Gideon's troubled soul, *". . . By the three hundred men that lapped will I save you, and deliver the Midianites into thine hand: and let all the other people go every man unto his place" (Judges 7:7).* "Gideon," God inferred, "I am fully aware of the exact number of men who have remained after the testing; I have counted them with you. However, I assure you that the few will be quite sufficient for the task. As I said to you before, you shall not die, for I shall save you. You will not need one more warrior – three hundred will certainly be enough for I am with you."

God's Will Is Never Frustrated

It made no difference to God whether the army was large or small; God was not depending on even three hundred to win the battle for Him. To the contrary, He so ordered the battle that each one of them had to completely and individually depend upon God in the battle and not on three hundred men massed around him. Not one of them would ever be able to say that it was by his own heroic deeds of battle that the victory was gained. God had said to Gideon, "I will save you," and save them He would. God had delivered His people into captivity, and it was God alone who would set them free.

Twenty-two thousand men had been afraid and slipped quietly home during the night. Nine thousand seven hundred were too full of their self-life and too little transformed by their faith in Jehovah to be trusted with this faith-demanding task. Only a small, dependent handful of untrained men remained. Nevertheless, they were men of faith, courage, and total commitment. Most important of all, they were chosen of God. "Fear not, Gideon," the Lord said, "with these men, I will save Israel."

As to those not chosen, each man returned to his own place. There was a place for each one – a place where he belonged. They were men who had responded to the call. God did not chastise, rebuke, or reprimand them; they simply had not measured up to His high standards for the battle. They had been measured and were found lacking – weighed and found deficient, for they had not been tried by the proving of men but by the infallible balance of Jehovah.

God was pleased to go against some half million men of the enemy army with only three hundred chosen and tried men. His chosen men would prove worthy to take the mighty, but unconventional, weapons of God and enter into the battle of the Lord.

# 20 …

Meat For Gideon's Men

"So the people took victuals in their hands, . . . and he sent all the rest of Israel every man unto his tent, and retained those three hundred men: and the host of Midian was beneath him in the valley" (Judges 7:8).

The Hebrew word for victuals implies "meat" of some kind. It also implies meat they had hunted and prepared by themselves. These divinely chosen ones were not the kind of men who would sit about indolently expecting Gideon to hand them a nicely cooked meal – well seasoned, garnished, and served on glazed porcelain. Neither did Gideon go out hunting game of some kind for his men. They were all in this battle together; every man of that company felt responsible for himself.

These valiant ones were men of the land; they were survivors. While others moaned and died of starvation, these men were alive and well. Oppression and adversity had developed them and honed their survival skills. Instead of destroying them and turning them into self-pitying beggars who fall easily into the pit of discouragement, their calamity became a ladder to abundant life. They were like jackals who snatch morsels of meat from the lion's prey.

The oppressive restrictions and malicious destruction inflicted upon these survivors by their conquerors had taught them how to live and grow strong on the land. Wise men they were; men who would not attempt to fight a battle without being well fortified by a plentiful portion of meat.

They knew of every edible plant, root, and fruit. They had located every rabbit warren and every deer trail. They had learned to hunt and provide meat and rich herbs for themselves and their families from the hills and valleys about them. They knew how to cunningly snare the hares as they ran through the thickets and to skillfully stalk the deer that roamed the hills. These men were quite able to provide sufficient victuals for themselves. They would face the battle with a full stomach and fight with well-fed strength.

Gideon had complained to the Angel that he could not feed an army even if he had one; he was far too poor and resourceless for such a feat. However, God never asked him to feed His chosen army, nor expected any help from Gideon's small stores. God chose men who could and would supply food for themselves.

God had already abundantly provided food for all of His chosen men in the well-watered fields and wooded hills that surrounded the well of Harod and in the small but steady stream that issued forth from that well.

God had chosen men:

. . . who knew how to gather food for their sustenance;

. . . educated in the strong school of hunger under the tutor called *strong adversity;*

. . . who knew how to use what God provided without whining;

. . . who did not sit around quaffing the ale of bitterness and the cup of self-pity;

. . . who in times of scarcity refused to go hungry but determined to find their own sustenance;

... who resolved to eat, live and not lay down and die – even though the time of abundance and plenty and the last revival was far behind them;

... who dared to defy the enemy instead of wallowing in defeat;

... who refused to give up their hope for better times and wait patiently for deliverance;

... who determined to walk when they could not run and wait if they could not walk;

... whose wings of faith were outspread and caught the first winds of revival;

... who would blow the trumpet as Gideon;

... who would be in the forefront of the next revival when the Lord sent again the times of refreshing.

Well-fed and well-supplied with water, these chosen men of God looked down on the enemy in the valley beneath them – not only beneath them in the valley below the hill at Harod's well, but also far beneath them in the realm of darkness as they looked down from the heights of Mount Faith-in-Jehovah upon which they firmly stood. The enemy was camped below in the valley of Fatal-Delusion, for they trusted in the help of the false gods, Baal and Chemosh, who in their silent, dumb helplessness could help no one at all.

Trumpets ... ? From Whence?

"And he divided the three hundred men into three companies, and he put a trumpet in every

man's hand, with empty pitchers, and lamps within the pitchers" (Judges 7:16).

Gideon put a ram's horn trumpet in every man's hand. How and from where Gideon procured three hundred trumpets out on the hill near the well of Harod we are not told. Three hundred trumpets would be hard to find in any city or village, let alone on a lonely hill far from any trumpet maker. The question remains unanswered – where did he find all those trumpets?

And how could Gideon have provided three hundred trumpets when he did not know beforehand that he would have exactly three hundred men in his army? We are not given the answer, but in some way, there was a miracle of Jehovah. We are only told that Gideon put a trumpet in every man's hand. We do know that Gideon believed in a miracle-working God, and in his simple one-track faith he expected God to miraculously give them victory. We also know God worked a tremendous miracle over nature in the affair of the fleeces. Was this then another miracle – God providing three hundred trumpets for Gideon to find in some cache?

It is most unrealistic for a peasant farmer-turned-warrior to arm himself with a trumpet as a weapon for war. An ox goad, a flail, a club, or an ax would be normal for farmers. But would a man bring a trumpet along to engage in a major battle? The source of the three hundred trumpets must remain hidden – just one more secret mystery in this amazing, miraculous revival of deliverance God worked for His people. We only know that from some puzzling unknown source – that defies any common solution – Gideon provided each man of his army with a trumpet.

Divine Strategy

Gideon remembered and pondered upon the word that God had given to Moses, "... *if ye go to war in your land against the enemy that oppresseth you, then ye shall blow an alarm with the trumpets; and ye shall be remembered before the Lord your God, and ye shall be saved from your enemies*" *(Numbers 10:9).*

His faith laid hold of that promise from God; in part it became the means that God would use to deliver them. Gideon said to himself, "Because God has instructed us to use trumpets in battle, we shall all have a trumpet, and we shall blow them valiantly before the Lord and call upon our God for help.

"The Midianites will hear us clearly declare our faith in our God as we call upon Him. Also, the sound will blow mind-boggling confusion and panic into Midianite ears. Jehovah shall hear our trumpets and know that we have put our trust in Him – not in our own strength of arms."

As the Spirit of Wisdom developed the revelation of God's strategy, faith for such a strategy grew in Gideon's heart and he laughed. He laughed so hilariously in joyful anticipation of victory that his men laughed with him there on the hilltop. "Those heathen Midianites cannot understand the mysterious ways of our God," he exulted. "They shall be perplexed by our victorious trumpets sounding forth our battle songs right in their faces.

"How astute! How enemy-baffling! How brilliant, ... yet how simple is Jehovah's plan!" mused Gideon. "Its wise simplicity will truly make us victorious. This will undoubtedly give us a wondrous success because the Midianites can never guess the super-bold delusion confronting them. We will need neither sword nor shield because we will not have to fight in this battle; Jehovah Shalom will fight for us."

Really the plan was very simple. They would surround the Midianite army, then blow their trumpets as if there was a vast army following their commander's trumpeters. Each one of them would stand as a trumpeter for a commander with a large battalion of fighters. They would hide their torches in their pitchers; then in the precise moment of utmost surprise, they would smash them to shards and let their torches blaze forth. The shining torches – as if to light the way for sword-wielding men behind them – plus all the noise their shouts and trumpets could make would utterly confuse and deceive the enemy. Gideon shouted aloud his praises to his Jehovah Shalom at the simplicity and victorious certainty of the plan that God revealed to him there on the hillside.

He could clearly see the astute yet simple wisdom. It would be a battle of nerves, of shock and confusion, of distrusting hysteria, of darkness and of panic for the Midianites. As for the men of Israel, they would be attacking with light, with courage, with faith, with the sound of their cries and with trumpets ever declaring their trust in God. Indubitably it would wreak blinding consternation in the minds of their enemies and mortal dread to their devil-gods.

Such has always been God's way to begin a new revival – the sounding of the trumpet to declare the faith for war, and the praise for God's faithfulness to His promises. When those trumpets sound out the powerful melodies, immediately confusion is brought to the enemy. Calls to the Throne of God in notes of faith and praise for divine intervention will release the divine light of victory for deliverance.

All Of One Accord

Each man had his own trumpet – all were the same kind of instruments. Each one gave forth the same certain sound that all could understand. Gideon's men were all of one faith, one purpose, and one mind; they would go out to battle as one man. Not one lacked his weapon of faith and praise, and all were experts in praising God with their trumpets – harmoniously they accompanied their prayer of faith.

They had heard the Voice of God's Spirit speaking through Gideon's trumpet, and these trumpet-armed men were ready. They did not need a crash course of concentrated practice on their trumpets. These were God's chosen men – men, not wimps. They were men of war, men of faith, and men of worship and praise. They were Triumphant Trumpeters for the Lord.

They were one in heart and one in mind with Gideon. As one man they would stand up and blow a daring challenge, praise their glorious God and voice the certain prophetic note of promised victory. They had gone beyond fear and feared not the consequences of their martial sound – it mattered not who heard them. Let their sound carry over into the valley; let the enemy know there stood men round about them who were not afraid – men who joyfully accepted the enemy's arrogant challenge with keen anticipation of triumphant victory. Let Baal and his vaunted minions from hell hear and tremble at the sound of fear-generating praises of Jehovah.

This band of three hundred men would run towards, not away from, battle. They were ready to sound the alarm of faith and in high praise prophesy the fall of the enemy that very day. Blowing the trumpet that all may hear was a daring declaration of faith in God; it called to arms the mighty, invincible armies of Heaven. When lips of faithful men would blow upon Israel's trumpets in battle, the hosts of God would attend the call.

Countless thousands of Jehovah's unseen warriors would be sent to join Gideon in the battle for Israel's deliverance.

The Angel of the Lord had promised to be with Gideon in this war, and He would listen for the sound of the trumpets. He would give them the promised deliverance.

The courageous three hundred would fearlessly inform the enemy that they were coming to regain the usurped dominions, defeat his army, capture his possessions, and utterly destroy him. Their note of faith would unmistakably declare their determination to fight the battle until victory. They could bravely proclaim their intentions because they had first heard God's promises in the secret place of their hearts.

The laughter and proclamations from the lips of these men on the mountain, echoed under the heavens and reverberated as dreadful decrees in the ears of God's enemies. Intuitively the enemy knew that their days had been numbered and had come to an end; their brave hearts melted in that knowledge. The shouts of joy and anticipated victory reached even into the valley of Jezreel and caused the Midianites to think that already some great army had arrived to help the Hebrews.

21

Men On The Mountaintop

Gideon's men impatiently waited on the hilltop with keen anticipation of the coming battle and expected victory. They rested serenely in the full assurance of the promises of God that came to them through Gideon. Although the Angel had not come to each one of them individually, they believed the report that Gideon brought to them. Their victorious Jehovah, the Mighty Man of War, was going to fight for them – He Himself had said so. This day He would break the bonds of oppressive tyranny that had so vexed them these past seven years. Because they believed the promises of God, they rejoiced in the envisioned success of the coming battle. Faith abided in them because revival had already begun in the hearts of the three hundred.

They were not oppressed or agitated with fearful expectations of deadly defeat. Faith in Jehovah gave them cheerful anticipation of the victory yet to come. Let the Midianites, the Amalekites, and the Ishmaelites gather together ever so vast a multitude in the magnitude of their wrath. The faith of God resident in these men rejoiced in the certainty that this vast horde would all fall before His small army. As their mighty God intervened and fought for them, they intended to shout the shout of victory. They were well aware that no enemy army in the world could stand against their all-powerful Jehovah. They were revivalists on their way to triumph. They were God's army marching to overcome the enemy that had lifted himself up against God and His people.

In the valley of Jezreel, lying beneath the brow of the hill where Gideon's small band of men waited, the multitude of the enemy host had spread their vast camp. God did not plan for the battle to be joined in the mountains because this would not be a hit and run, guerilla-type battle. The plan of God was to face the enemy with full confrontation in order to defeat them once and for all. The well of Harod on the hill would not be their battleground; it was only the place of preparation, of strengthening, of hearing God's instructions and encouragements to their faith.

He would send His three hundred men of faith out from the comparative safety of the mountaintop and down into the valley – down into the very camp of the enemy to fight the battle face to face. Fear they did not, for they possessed the promise of Jehovah as their strong defense. He would be their shield and their buckler. They knew that the Presence of the Lord that had covered them on the heights would go with them down into the valley and into the battle.

"Get Thee Down"

As the evening shadows grew long and began to obscure the horizon and darkness began to possess the earth, the Lord commanded Gideon and his courageous three hundred. *"And it came to pass the same night, that the Lord said unto him, 'Arise, get thee down unto the host; for I have delivered it into thine hand'" (Judges 7:9).*

"Gideon," God instructed, "there will be no more delay. You will not have to wait any longer; I will give you the victory this very night. The battle will be fought in the darkness in the valley. You will not need anymore time to prepare. The Midianites will be sleeping in their futile imagination of safety, but they rest in vain this night. They have put their trust in the strength of their numbers, their weapons, and their gods, but this night shall their arrogant souls stand in judgment before Me whom they have despised. Fear not, but make ready to attack them in their sleep for I shall deliver them all to you."

What a strong confirming word to the faith of the three hundred. Their brief time of waiting was over. The time of their oppression and humiliation at the hands of the Midianites would terminate suddenly ere the morning dawned. They were to arise and go into battle before the sun ever rose upon the Midianite host.

God said to Gideon, "I HAVE delivered them into your hand." In the invisible world of the Eternal God, deliverance had already taken place. As far as God was concerned, it was a completed battle; the defeat of Midian was already accomplished. He had victory all worked out ahead of time. He had returned the wall of protection to His own people – a wall which no spear or sword could penetrate. The ancient separating wall – the wall of light and fire that God raised between the Egyptian host and Moses' fleeing Hebrew slaves – had returned to protect Gideon and his band from their enemies.

God's foreordained time for the enemy's occupation of Israel was fulfilled; His clock had sounded out the hour of their freedom. The iron fist of cruel, malevolent Midian had finally beaten His people out of their foolishness and caused them to turn back to their true and living God. The malicious forces of destruction and evil were again placed under the irresistible restriction of the sovereign restraint of God. All-wise foreknowledge considered the battle and ensuing deliverance was already executed. That very night, God's innumerable angelic host in fiery ranks stood poised, eager, and armed with their terrible flaming two-edged swords.

Before the dawn of morning's light broke over the plains of Jezreel, the battle would be all over, the spoil would be waiting for collection and the captives would all be set free. God's implacable enemies would never more see the light of day nor the light of eternity, but outer darkness would be their habitation forever.

"Listen To The Enemy"

However, considering the weakness of human flesh and its limitations, God knew some trepidations were still harassing Gideon's heart. In Gideon's world of flesh and blood there was a fearsome contest ahead with a powerful enemy. His faith had overcome his fears; he would not turn back now. But God wanted His captain to be more-than-conqueror in this battle. Although Gideon did not ask for anymore signs or proof of victory, God in His loving, all-wise wisdom offered to His servant yet another impressive assurance to lift his faith into still greater heights.

> **" 'Gideon,' God said, '. . . if thou fear to go down, go thou with Phurah thy servant down to the host: And thou shalt hear what they say; and afterward shall thine hands be strengthened to go down unto the host.' Then went he down with Phurah his servant unto the outside of the armed men that were in the host" (Judges 7:10-11).**

"Go down the hill, Gideon. Draw near to their camp and listen to what the enemy is saying one to another. Go, listen to their whisperings and secret mutterings. Listen carefully and see that I have already begun to deliver them into your hands. I have troubled their hearts with frightening dreams and have sent the spirit of fear into their midst. They are trembling in dread already as they await your attack perhaps on the morrow; for they know not when the battle will be joined. I shall surprise them this night before the morrow comes. They believe in Jehovah your God – they believe and tremble. In the depths of their rebellion and hatred, they ever refuse to repent and cry to the Lord for mercy.

"As you listen, you will discover that the enemy is an inveterate liar; he loudly shouts his threatening and mouths fearful words of retribution and destruction to you. But when you hear what he says in secret, you will find it is quite another matter. Go, listen carefully and hear what the enemy whispers in secret.

"If you are fearful, you will find that the enemy is a thousandfold more fearful. They all fear your God, your light, and your revived faith in Jehovah. Your cries of intercessions and the trumpet's voice of your praises have caused their limbs to tremble and their hearts to melt within them. Fainthearted, they anticipate defeat. The sword of the Lord wielded in the lips of His sons has pierced their ears — so go down and see for yourself and listen to them."

A Dream Of Barley Bread

"And the Midianites and the Amalekites and all the children of the east lay along in the valley like grasshoppers for multitude; and their camels were without number, as the sand by the sea side for multitude" (Judges 7:12).

As Gideon looked down on the enemy camp, it looked endless; it covered acres and acres – from approximately six hundred to a thousand acres of land. Sprawled out below them, the encampment of the enemy monopolized the whole valley. What a sight to inspire fear! They were like a plague of grasshoppers covering the ground – as uncountable as the trees in the forests of Lebanon. However, as Gideon crept down the steep hill and approached the enemy camp, the immensity of the multitude shrank in his immediate vision to a more acceptable number.

Vision, limited in the darkness, put things in the right perspective for faith to hold strong. How gracious of the Lord to use darkness to hide the apparent power of the enemy! The power of the enemy was but an empty show – a threatening noise and a deceitful intimidation – which lacked the power of substance and truth.

To reveal the hidden truth of reality unto Gideon, God had sent a dream to one of the enemy soldiers while he fitfully slept. When Gideon noiselessly drew near and listened, he heard that soldier apprehensively relate his frightening dream to a companion. *"Listen," he said, "I have just had a dream: To my surprise, a loaf of barley bread tumbled into the camp of Midian; it came to a tent and struck it so that it fell and overturned, and the tent collapsed" (The word, tumbled, in Hebrew means "came like a whirlwind") (Judges 7:13).*

To Gideon's amazement he heard the other soldier gasp out in horror as he gave his answer and interpretation of his fellow soldier's dream, *"This is nothing else but the sword of Gideon the son of Joash, a man of Israel; for into his hand God has delivered Midian and the whole camp" (Judges 7:14).*

"Jehovah has delivered Midian and all his host into Gideon's hand. We are lost; we are defeated and destroyed," he moaned. "We will never see our homes or families again. Why did we ever do such a foolhardy thing as to attack the Israelites after we heard of their revival, their return to worship of Jehovah and their repudiation of Baal? We should have made peace with them then and there instead of going to war.

"I feared this would happen when we dared to fight against Jehovah's people after they repented, left our gods and returned to their powerful God. Do they not call Gideon, Jerubaal ("Let Baal fight against him")? We should have known when our Baal kept silence and rose not in vengeance against Gideon that our cause was lost and our gods afrighted.

"We are fools and our leaders also; they thought we could get away with it in spite of Israel's Jehovah. We were deceived with our hate; like blind simpletons we believed we could destroy the heritage of Jehovah with impunity and smash their resistance as one shatters a clay pot.

"This is our just reward for our cruel ways. Would to Baal that we had been merciful to them when they were under our dominion. Then they would have continued their worship of Baal and not have returned to their terrible Jehovah. Midian is destroyed, our wives and children will be killed or enslaved, and our possessions taken. O Baal, I know you cannot help – you have no strength against Jehovah. We are dead men. Our wives, our sons, and daughters will never see our faces again!

"Alas! Alas! We are fallen this day never to rise again. Their Almighty Jehovah, who destroyed the powerful Egyptians and all the Canaanite kings, has risen against us and we are doomed for there is none to save us. All the host of three nations cannot save us from the vengeance of their mighty God, Jehovah.

"Jehovah has arisen in His wrath, and His sword is unsheathed against us. Who can stand against Him? Who can fight against His flaming sword? Gideon shall descend upon us like a whirlwind from the desert, and we shall be carried away as dust before it. He shall sweep over us like a tornado and destroy us in tempestuous fury. Woe! Woe, be upon us for Midian is defeated! Not one of our gods can protect us against their great all-powerful God."

Gideon listened in amazement as the interpretation fell like a sentence of doom from the dreaming soldier's companion. Already the terrorizing fear of Jehovah had possessed their hearts. He knew that such fear in an army would set them up for certain defeat.

Gideon, God's barley cake, knew that he was a cake well baked and ready – the hot fires of the oven of adversity and the flames from the altar on the rock had baked him into a destroying cake which God would throw into their camp with the fury of a tornado. God's cake of barley bread, Gideon, would tumble into their mist like a thundering hurricane of God's wrath. God would use His own prepared barley bread to smite them and knock their tents into the dust from whence they came.

Terror And Consternation

The enemy had been shivering in fear ever since that mighty trumpet blast echoed and reverberated throughout the valley – even before they gathered for battle. Just the anointed blast of Gideon's trumpet alone had filled their hearts with dismay and dreadful trembling. No one could ever blow a blast like that unless the Presence of God's Spirit were upon him.

Nevertheless, in their prideful rebellion and arrogant confidence, they thought that if they enlarged their numbers with the armies of the Amalakites and Ishmaelites, and thereby multiplied their arms and their gods, surely they could overcome Gideon and his God.

It had given them so much pleasure to persecute the children of Jehovah. In their lust of malicious hatred, they had delighted in torturing, harassing, and killing those Hebrews who represented the religion of Jehovah. They were not willing to allow any revival of that hated religion to rise again and bring that hated Jehovah into the land. They thought they had beaten belief in Jehovah all out of them already – what an entertainment it had been to torment the Israelites and hear them cry and scream. They did not want to lose that morbid fun.

The Midianites' hatred of God and their enjoyment of persecution overcame their prudence. Even though they heard that revival had begun and that fearful Jehovah had returned to His people, their confidence in their own strong arm overruled their discretion. They foolishly chose to go to war rather than surrender.

The Midianites could not erase from their minds the terrible defeat their nations had already suffered at the hands of Moses and God's anointed people. The stories of the mighty acts of Jehovah in Egypt, when He had delivered His people, arose in their minds like horrid specters in the night. Nevertheless, in rash rebellion they called on the Amalekites and the Ishmaelites to help them – as if numbers could save them from Jehovah's mighty arm.

However enormous as the multitude of their army was, they were hopelessly doomed. Now belatedly, they realized the enormity of their foolhardy decision. All the power of their armed might could in no way save them from the wrath of the dreadful Jehovah of the Israelites who had returned to Gideon and his army.

As Gideon listened to the words of his terrorized enemy, every harassing worry vanished as smoke in the air. Faith soared on eagle wings, even higher than was needed for the deliverance of God's people. He returned to his waiting men with faith amplified; he was eager to begin the battle. He felt like he was walking ten feet tall and his enemies were all pygmies.

"By my God I can run through this troop of three armies. I can leap over the wall of armed might for Jehovah, our own true God, has given us the victory. We shall not die of starvation; no longer will we cringe in fear of our neighbors. The Midianites shall be grist for our mills and chaff under our feet! Our time of humiliation and affliction has passed for our God has heard our cry and has come down to deliver us out of their hands," sang Gideon in a psalm of praise and exaltation.

22

The Sword Of Gideon

"It is the sword of Gideon!" the frightened Midianite warrior had cried. But Gideon did not own a sword of steel because the Midianites had absolutely prohibited the Israelites from making or having a sword in their possession on pain of death. Precisely then, what manner of sword was the terrified brain of that Midianite seeing?

Gideon had no sword? Ah, but yes indeed, Gideon did have a sword. Not a sword made of fine damascus steel . . . nor even one of well forged iron, but Gideon had the Sword of the Lord, the living irrevocable Word of Jehovah from the lips of God's Messenger from Heaven. His sword was so swift that no living creature could possibly escape it; it was so sharp that the finest armor had no defense against it.

> *"For the word of God is `quick, and powerful, and sharper than any two-edged sword, piercing even to the dividing asunder of soul and spirit, and of the joints and marrow, and is a discerner of the thoughts and intents of the heart" (Hebrews 4:12).*

God gave Gideon His sword the day he offered his sacrifice on the rock before the Angel. Also, on that day Jehovah Shalom opened Gideon's spiritual ears that he might hear the word from God directly in his spirit. That sword would not only destroy the horde of pagan Midianites but also all the invisible enemies that accompanied and ruled over them. Those invisible princes of darkness were only too well acquainted with the sword's unlimited, dreadful power. Although Gideon's sword was invisible to natural eyes, nevertheless, it was horribly visible to the unseen forces that accompanied the Midianite army.

It is curious indeed that the enemy soldier feared Gideon's sword, seeing he had no visible sword forged by man in his hands. Probably the enemy reasoned that Gideon had made a bargain with the Syrians or the Egyptians, and that their armies had come to help him. It was utterly beyond the Midianites' comprehension that men could actually have a God so wonderful, so powerful, and so helpful as to come help man in an hour of crisis or need. Much as they feared Jehovah, they still could not believe in Him being a God willing and able to intervene for men of faith.

The Adversaries

The unseen enemies of Israel shivered and quaked at the thought of another powerful weapon of Gideon visible to their spectral eyes – his faith in the word of God. They knew and dreaded the irresistible, destructive power of the sword of the Spirit, the word of God, when wielded by the arm of faith.

Against that sharp two-edged sword – a flaming devouring fire in the mouth of God's chosen vessel – the enemy had neither shield, defense, nor refuge. The adversaries of God's children have never yet devised a way to deflect or avoid the thrusts of that deadly weapon. Inevitably it will draw black blood from those malicious adversaries every time it is brandished. *"'Is not My word like as a fire?' saith the Lord; 'and like a hammer that breaketh the rock in pieces'" (Jeremiah 23:29)?*

More often than they liked to remember, Israel's adversaries – the demons of their idol-gods – had crossed swords with men of faith and had been miserably defeated by that divine weapon. They had felt the mortal pain of its dreadful destroying wound when wielded by the hands of Moses in Egypt. They had writhed in hellish torment and ignominiously had fallen when Joshua picked up that sword at the walls of Jericho. They had felt its dreaded power more than once when Othniel, Ehud, and Deborah the prophetess valiantly had picked it up and brandished it on high. To their bitter shame and pain, they had learned the irresistibly destructive power of that sword of the living Word of the Lord. How they trembled every time they heard it unsheathed!

From Boyhood To Valiant Manhood

God had transformed the questioning youth – the rebellious young harvester, Gideon of the tribe of Manassah – into His valiant vessel of faith called Jerubaal (Baal's overthrower). God made the rebel Gideon into a man of obedience, of faith, of valor, and of war. God loves His babies; He patiently takes time to raise His boys; He persistently trains His young men; but ever His desire is to produce men of valor, men of war, and overcomers.

Once again, a man who believed in Jehovah, the true and living God, had arisen in Israel. God made a man who not only received His word but also determined to obey it. Gideon dared to grasp the hilt of that sword, the word of God, with his hand of faith and fearlessly unsheathe it in battle. He would wage war with the enemies that lived in his own back garden.

The Midianites knew the enslaved Israelites could not possibly be delivered by the mere strength of Gideon's arm, however skillfully he might wield a sword. If that were all they had to contend with in that battle, they would not have been filled with terror. But they feared the victorious exploits of Jehovah, Israel's God – exploits that amply adorned the pages of history.

Only a century prior to this battle their own ancestors had the sad experience of fighting with Israel's God. How easily He had delivered them into the hand of Israel by the power of His fiery two-edged sword. And every Midianite man or woman was well aware of the history of that lost war with Jehovah's people.

The terrified, conscience-stricken Midianites thoroughly feared what the Righteous King of all the universe would do to them in swift retribution for their wickedness. Once His almighty arm was made bare and His dreadful, fiery sword unsheathed, they – who had shown no mercy to Israel – would now receive no mercy.

The Midianite warrior's dream accurately revealed that God would hurl His "barley cake" into their camp with the force of a deadly tornado. Without warning and without escape, they would be destroyed by the strength of God's right arm. Jesus taught the divine principle saying, *"Blessed are the merciful: for they shall obtain mercy" (Matthew 5:7)*. But where no mercy had been shown, the Divine Judge would show no mercy in the day of judgment.

"God Is With Me"

With revival now in his heart, Gideon knew that God would not give him faith, courage, weapons, and an army, and then leave him to fight the battle alone. He expectantly believed that the mighty Presence of his Jehovah would accompany him into the very camp of the enemy. God's Presence, he well knew, would produce an awesome, demoralizing fear in the hearts of the wicked.

Gideon knew he would fight this battle without sword of steel or shield of bronze. He would rely solely on the orders of Jehovah Shalom. In the silent night the Midianites would be absolutely paralyzed and terrorized by the shock, the confusion, and the sound of blaring trumpets and shattered pitchers. Rudely intruding into the calm silence of their tranquil sleep, the fright generating blast of the triumphant trumpets ordering the unseen host into battle would stampede them into mortal and bewildering disarray just as lightning bolts will stampede a herd of buffaloes on the prairie.

Their flaming torches would dazzlingly shine in the face of the enemy, magnified immeasurably by the fiery wrath emanating from the face of Jehovah. At the same time, God would send the searing effulgence of invisible flames of divine judgment blazing into the Midianites' brains. The manifestation of His terrible and dreadful Presence would bewilder His idolatrous enemies.

Not By Might

Israel's deliverance would not come as the result of winning an ordinarily pitched battle, in which many would fall and die on both sides. The steel of Israel would not clash with the iron and steel of Midian. This battle would not be won by the arm of flesh, by the force of numbers or by ferocious military skill as the forces locked in mortal combat. Instead, in the light of his inspired faith, Gideon saw that his God intended to utterly destroy Israel's enemies.

The powerful, fiery two-edged sword of Jehovah would be unsheathed to win this war. The debilitating awful rays from His countenance would bring blinding confusion and hopeless panic. Stupefying terror and the eternal darkness of death would fall upon the arrogant, God-defiant host of the Midianites.

Because the host of Jehovah's invisible army of angels would be ever present at their side, not a single sword thrust or wound would be received by any of God's little three hundred strong army. The enemy would not even be able to come against them; not a single one would receive a wound. The threatening might of the Midianite army – fully invincible in the natural – would utterly fail because the God-given faith in Gideon would unleash the powers of the eternal, all-powerful Jehovah and His immutable word.

When the Angel visited Gideon under the old oak tree, it was the sign that the gracious favor of Jehovah their God had returned to abide with and deliver His people from their galling oppression. From that moment on, revival . . . wonderful delivering revival . . . had come to Israel. As in all revivals, some would open their hearts to God more than others. Nevertheless, God had sent again His mercies to His suffering people and the whole land would enjoy deliverance from their oppression. Jehovah had graciously turned back to them His countenance of peace. The time of divine judgment upon their malevolent enemies had come, and with that, the time of liberation had come for the remnant of God's people.

23

Gideon Worshiped

Gideon listened in amazed delight as his enemies admitted their terror of the "barley-cake" tumbling into their midst and their calling it Gideon. He realized the Midianite army had already surrendered to the fear of Jehovah; fearful anticipation had dismayed them. As the final step in the preparation of his faith, God gave Gideon the knowledge of the demoralized condition of the Midianite. Soon Gideon would go into battle fearlessly and would courageously trust in his God alone. The God of Peace had overcome all of Gideon's fears and doubts. Gideon laughed to himself as he thought, "With all appearances to the contrary, the truth is that all the advantages in this war are on my side."

However, in spite of this wonderful information cheering his soul, the first thing Gideon did was not to run immediately back to his band and share this latest news of the Midianite's dread of coming defeat. Neither did he begin to order his men into battle formation. In the amazing wonder of all that Jehovah had done and all that He was going to do for him, Gideon took time out to worship his Jehovah Shalom there on the hillside alone. His heart overflowed with gratitude and amazed thankfulness. In but a few hours, his God had miraculously brought him from being only a discouraged peasant vassal into the realization that he was truly God's chosen leader who would march at the head of the triumphant army that would defeat all their enemies.

Gideon felt it absolutely necessary to delay the battle a little while longer to take prime time to worship Jehovah Shalom. In the strength of his God-given faith, Gideon had adjusted his priorities. First and most importantly, he would take time to worship. Gideon was in battle readiness; time was at a premium with dawn only a few hours away. Nevertheless, Gideon paused and worshiped his wonderful Jehovah in the strength of his reborn, revived faith.

"And it was so, when Gideon heard the telling of the dream, and the interpretation thereof, that he worshiped, and returned into the host of Israel, and said, 'Arise; for the Lord hath delivered into your hand the host of Midian'" (Judges 7:15).

In spite of the pressure of time and the keen desire to give the orders to start the battle . . . in spite of the anticipation of harvesting the spoils and the glorious deliverance that awaited them . . . in spite of the glories of victory that awaited him, the swelling gratitude in Gideon's heart impelled him to first pour out his heart in thankful praise and adoring worship to Jehovah.

Gideon had first felt the Spirit of worship arise in his heart when he met the Angel at the altar on the rock and the heavenly fire flamed upon his offering. Then he again felt the Spirit of worship following the glorious revelation of Jehovah Shalom and of pardon. Then and there he built an altar unto the God of Israel as the newborn revival fervor brought the Spirit of worship into his soul. Gideon had learned the importance of worship of the Lord his God, and Gideon became a true worshiper of Jehovah.

In the Spanish language Bible, the word for worship is translated "adoration". To adore is stronger than to like; to adore is more intense than to love. To worship means to adore, i.e., to concentrate one's whole being in an outpouring of love and gratitude from the inmost heart unto God.

Worship Was . . .

. . . Worship was Moses prophetically singing "The Song of Moses and the Lamb" – the song of deliverance at God's triumph on the shores of the Red Sea.

. . . Worship was Gideon in faith – on the eve of the most miraculous battle in history – setting aside time to pour out his soul in wonder and gratitude.

. . . Worship was Hannah in the tabernacle committing her only begotten and dearly loved son, Samuel, unto God and leaving him there with Eli the priest.

. . . Worship was David pouring out unto God the water too precious to drink because it was brought at the price of blood from Bethlehem's well by his mighty men.

. . . Worship was Jeremiah's flowing river of tears as the compassionate sorrow in his heart dared to plead for mercy.

. . . Worship was Mary's soul singing the Great Magnificat, "My soul doth magnify the Lord, and my spirit hath rejoiced in God my Savior."

. . . Worship was Mary breaking the alabaster box that represented her self-life and pouring out its fragrance in surrendered love upon the feet of Jesus.

. . . Worship was John reclining on the breast of Jesus at the mystical last supper – just resting in that heavenly Presence.

. . . Worship was Mary Magdalene weeping in heartbroken sorrow for her missing Lord at the tomb on resurrection morn.

Worship In Faith

Jehovah Shalom had graciously and tenderly manifested His grace upon Gideon; He had chosen him and fully confirmed His word to him. Gideon's heart was simply overcome in gratitude and love to the God who had given him the revelation of His own divine heart of love and mercy in this victorious hour. The wonder of it all! The miraculous and mysterious ways of his God and the certainty of the outcome of the battle swept over Gideon's soul in a wave of adoration.

Gideon believed God. He doubted not that God would give them victory that very night. He had no fearful anticipation that the morning messengers would race out to the impoverished people hiding in their dens and caves with the disconsolate proclamation, "Hear all about *The Suicidal Charge* of Gideon and his three hundred. Hear how the fanatical Jehovah Shalom *CULT* has been deplorably defeated. Run for your lives! Hide yourselves where you can for the victorious Midianites are coming to requite malicious vengeance."

To the contrary, Gideon was certain that on the morrow, long before sun went down, they would proclaim the glorious tidings of Jehovah's mighty deliverance in joyful accents. Ecstatic rejoicing would ring throughout all Israel. New songs would be sung with exuberant dances and jubilant rejoicing.

Gideon Anticipates Triumph

As Gideon worshiped in the reverent stillness of the night around him, his soaring God-inspired faith released all the ways and means of the coming battle into the capable hands of his mighty Jehovah. God would be their Captain and He would order their strategy.

Gideon arose from his time of worship prostrate on the ground feeling as if the heart of a lion had been placed within him. As divine fervor inspired him to press on to the battle, he was ready to tear into his enemies as meat for his prey. For as he worshiped there, God had slipped into his mind the next order, *"Arise; for the Lord hath delivered into your hand the host of Midian" (Judges 7:15).* Gideon knew that the hour had come for action.

When Gideon returned to the valiant three hundred waiting on the mountaintop, he gave them the same mighty command Jehovah had given him: "The moment of triumph has come! God has given us the victory. Arise, let us go forth in His Name this night and see the triumph of our own Jehovah.

"Fear not, for in this battle you will see the irresistible flaming sword of the Lord destroy His enemies. It will not be by our clever fighting, extraordinary tactics, superhuman strength, or cunning strategy that this battle will be won. Therefore, we will win this victory by the mighty arm of the God of Israel, and unto Him shall be all the glory. We all know this battle is impossible for us by our puny power, but Almighty Jehovah is with us. We have but to arise and go down into the valley; Jehovah is waiting there to give us the victory."

To God Be The Glory

Gideon had truly understood the Angel's implied message, "Keep no glory for yourself." The Angel had also said, "Pour out the broth also on the rock." He must make no attempt to get personal glory from God's miracle power. Gideon intended to give unto God the glory due unto Him. There would be no published accolades of Gideon's prowess – no ambitious building up a kingdom for his own glory. There would be no dynasty established for the family of Gideon. God alone would have all the glory.

Gideon's awesome encounter with the Angel of God had humbled him to the very border of death. But gracious Jehovah had raised him up from the terror-filled abyss of his sinful state that was revealed to him when the Angel had shined light into his soul. Only the revelation of God as Jehovah Shalom (Peace) had revived hope and brought pardon to his lost soul, but the fear of the Lord remained in him. He was not about to rise and offend that mighty Jehovah Shalom by seeking the glory for himself.

Confidently waiting for his return to the mountaintop, the men were elated to hear Gideon call out, "Arise, it is time to go before the morning comes upon us. Now is the time of salvation! Now is the accepted time! Arise before the night is over and the dawn breaks for we shall be free men. Arise warriors of Jehovah, arise in His mighty Name! You have been chosen and prepared for this transcendent hour. Gird on your mystic weapons of mighty power. Let us go forth in haste for victory draws nigh."

As his eager men stood about him in the cool darkness, Gideon shared with them the plan of battle as God had revealed it to him – a plan that has never been used before in battle, nor has ever been used since. This strategy was so simple, yet so absurdly daring. In the annals of all the thousands of battles fought in the world, never has one been known where a handful of men destroyed a mighty army of hundreds of thousands of trained warriors. Their strategy was their strange but conquering weapons, . . . a trumpet, . . . a torch, . . . and a pitcher.

24

Divided They Will Conquer

Gideon carefully explained to his men the peculiar and unconventional battle strategy given him by God, and his little valiant army was eager to follow it implicitly. "Hallelujah, that will work," they said. "It is ingenious, it is so simple, and it is so impossible that the Midianites will never guess the magnitude of the charade. They will be utterly deceived and fall for our ruse like a fish for a worm." In simple trust the chosen three hundred believed God. They rejoiced when Gideon gave them the shrewd, simple, audacious plan for overcoming the Midianites. The daring faith which God had developed in their leader inspired these zealous men to follow Gideon straight into battle.

They were also much encouraged in their faith when they heard Gideon's report of the dream of the "barley cake" hurled into the midst of the enemy's camp. They realized the paralyzing effect of fear and knew that half the battle was won already.

Gideon's troops were not trained in any of the arts of warfare; they had never practiced marching in step in drill or parade, and they had never been through boot camp. Nevertheless, they were men who would obey orders without questions.

Gideon explained their plan and how they would put their plan into action, "We will divide ourselves into three companies of one hundred men, each under three leaders. We will creep down quietly and carefully into the valley while the Midianites are sleeping. However, keep in mind that any noise or loud misstep can give us all away. Starting now, we will have time to be in place while it is still dark, but we must hurry and keep moving.

"As we head down the hill, one company will go to the right towards the upper end of the valley where the open field lies. The second company will go behind them to the low narrow end of the valley on the left. The third will go with me and we will slip up on them from across the valley on the high side. That high cliff they are camped up against for safety will hold them in on this side. We must separate individually in the valley and so distance ourselves one from the other that we completely surround the whole camp on the three open sides.

"Once we are all in place, close up to the borders of their camp, we will suddenly arise upon them from all three sides at once – shouting and acting as if we were an immense army. Each one of you will act as if you were trumpeters and light givers to three hundred army captains with thousands of valiant troops following closely behind you. The enemy will be deceived by our actions and believe that an immense army of trained warriors are following your trumpeted orders. In the darkness, our enemies will be totally confused and think they are ambushed and surrounded on all sides by a great army they cannot see.

"Of course, you realize that this encampment is so large it will require us to be completely separated one from the other. Each man will be separated by fifty cubits or more from his brother on either side. We must make sure that we completely surround them as an immense army would and give them no avenue to escape. We will corral them as a flock of sheep in the meadow are corralled by one lone sheepdog.

"We will time and synchronize our attack by the stars as they cross the sky. You must all be in your appointed place by the time you see that lone bright star overhead cross the top of that high promontory of rocks on the hilltop on the west. Although each one of you will be alone, nevertheless, we must suddenly and simultaneously attack them all at once shouting and trumpeting as if we were an innumerable host surrounding them.

"But being separated does not mean each one fights on his own. The strength of our strategy is that we work so completely as one man that they will be fooled into thinking we are many. I believe we will not have to fight them at all. Jehovah will fight for us and turn every man's sword against his neighbor in the darkness and in their total confusion.

"Because they will think that a powerful army has come into their camp, they will recklessly fight whoever is near at hand in the darkness and confusion. In their fright and bewilderment, anyone that approaches them they will take for an enemy. We will light amongst them like a fox in a henyard, and they will go around fighting in circles like a millstone, not knowing which way to go.

"Do What You See Me Do"

"You will be alone in the darkness, but you must be very alert as to what I do. Immediately, each one of you must do exactly the same as I do. I will be leading my men from the high end across the valley and will approach the camp from where you see the shadow of that large clump of willow trees there on the far side from where we are standing now.

"When I blow the trumpet, all three hundred of you blow your trumpets with all your might sounding out Israel's marching orders. Then when I smash my pitcher and let my torch blaze into light, you must immediately and noisily shatter your pitchers and let your torches suddenly erupt in brilliant flame in the moonless night. And when I shout our shout of victory in the name of our mighty Jehovah, then you shout also with all your voice and we will splinter the still night with our trumpets and war cries.

Divided, Yet United

Although each man was separated far from each other and could not see the other in the darkness, yet they were all united in their common objective and understanding. As solidly joined together as three hundred branches on Gideon's solitary oak tree, they trusted each one his fellow, and each had full confidence in their leader, Gideon, and in the command God had given him.

Gideon's men were ready to follow him into what could be certain death, but they were rich in faith in Jehovah's promises of deliverance. They were ready and willing to follow those most unconventional military orders – orders that seemed to literally invite the sword, arrow, and spear of the enemy directly into their own illuminated faces.

The human impossibility of winning such a one-sided battle before them, caused them to increase their trust and dependency upon God. It never occurred to them to complain or cavil over having to obey such bizarre orders. Knowing that God was going to fight for them, they trusted that any method of attack He would give would surely be successful.

Mystery Weapons Distributed

"Now here are your weapons," said Gideon as he gave to each man a trumpet, a pitcher, and a torch. "We will blow our trumpets from all points around their camp. We will play the orders to charge for all the supposed hosts of warriors behind us. At the same time, we will shout loudly our battle cry and praise Jehovah our mighty God.

Simultaneously, we will all break our pitchers with a thunderous crash. Then our torches will blaze into light as if there were tens of thousands of men behind us following our light into battle. All this noise and confusion around them on all sides will frighten our enemies into mortal panic. They will be dazzled like a covey of partridges at night – blinded by the light and easily picked up from the ground. Easy prey these Midianites will be for us."

Where and how Gideon obtained three hundred trumpets, pitchers, and torches in that short a time is truly an intriguing mystery. It must have been a wondrous miracle of some kind, in order for Gideon to have such a large supply of those unusual items on hand to give his men for the battle – three hundred pitchers were in one pile, three hundred rams' horns prepared into trumpets were in another and three hundred torches lay in yet another. Truly it is a mystery how they got them all. One wishes that the scribe who wrote this history for us would have felt inspired to write how and in what manner Gideon procured his exotic weapons out there in the hills – especially in such a short time.

Each man was given a torch that he must somehow manage to keep burning and hidden within the pitchers. That in itself is quite a mystery. Normally, the lack of oxygen in the pitchers would quickly extinguish the lighted torches; by the time each soldier finally broke open the closed pitcher, the torch would have gone out. But, if on the other hand, the pitchers were open, then the light would shine out in the darkness and alert the sentinels of the Midianite camp of their approach. How could they have kept the fire burning in a pitcher so designed that no light could escape to betray them in the dark night? We are not told their secret, but we do know that they were successful in their enterprise. No light escaped until the pitchers were broken; the light was all secretly hidden inside those earthen pitchers until the precise moment of release.

Surely those hidden torches represented the flame of faith and revival which was burning in their own hearts. They themselves were like unto the clay pitchers – on the outside it appeared that nothing was taking place and life continued as usual, but hidden inside was a light-fire burning and waiting the order for release unto battle.

Weapons like these had never been used before in any of the many battles Israel had fought. Furthermore, never again was a war to be won with such unwarlike articles in the hands of peasant soldiers. Their weapons were completely alien to ordinary warfare. They were so unique that the Midianites never dreamed of them or the power of them. Rather than powerful weapons of decisive victory in the hands of men of mighty faith, they appeared as toys in the hands of a deluded army of fools.

Their exceptional power was in the element of shock-surprise they would produce in the enemy. They would terribly magnify the fear already in the hearts of the Midianites. The stupefying fright they already had, plus the strategic tactics of a surprise ambush in the night, would bring total bewildering disorientation to the Midianite army. They would inevitably believe they were attacked by an innumerable army of trained soldiers Israel had hired somewhere.

The weapons they carried into battle had not the power to either wound or kill a single person, but Gideon believed that God himself would destroy the enemy using their own swords of cruelty. These strange items were the only weapons God had chosen for Gideon to use in this battle, they had no other.

Weapons Not Carnal But Mighty

No other weapons . . . ? Ah, well . . . . Yes, . . . they did have other weapons, mighty weapons. First of all they were well covered and protected with the impenetrable shield of faith – a defensive refuge behind which they were as safe as if they rested by their own fireside.

Then, as they marched in unison in the power of obedience to God, the sharp pointed spear of the fearful sound of praise to their own God, Jehovah, pricked the ears of the enemy with sharp terror. Those praises, like sharp fire-arrows, penetrated the enemies' brains and so unhinged their rationality and judgment that they went about like insane persons killing each other – be it friend or brother.

Oh yes, . . . they did have one sword, but only one in all their small company. But what a sword! It was the flaming two-edged sword of their mighty Jehovah that turned every which way in absolute obedience to the Divine Will and Word. It would be drenched in the blood of His enemies ere it was sheathed and the night was over.

In truth, their weapons would prove so effective in battle that not a man of Gideon's company would be wounded in the fray. The Midianite army would be overcome and destroyed by the weapons which were mighty. *"For the weapons of our warfare are not carnal, but mighty through God to the pulling down of strongholds"* (2 Corinthians 10:4).

Gideon and his men trusted implicitly in these strange weapons; they deemed them sufficient to win the battle. God did not provide them with spears, swords, or shields, but the weapons God provided for them proved to be wondrously effective.

God had selected exceptional men for He had in mind exceptional weapons. He knew those whom He had chosen would have the will, the skill, and the necessary level of obedience in faith to use His choice of arms.

Utterly Irrational

No doubt an armchair general of that day or any captain in King Saul's army would be amazed and horrified at such a scheme of battle. The very idea of using such weapons against such suicidal odds in attacking so many well-armed and experienced soldiers was hare-brained – if not down right madness.

Imagine some modern day general using such laughable weapons as trumpets, clay pitchers, and torches against hundreds of thousands of well-armed, trained warriors in today's wars. Surely, to the natural mind it was utter foolishness and to be absolutely condemned. It would be considered outright suicidal and reckless self-destruction by today's generals trained at West Point Military Academy.

The carnal man might ask, "Would God send His warriors into battle with such inadequate weapons?" But what things the carnal mind of man considers apropos and adequate are immeasurably different from what God considers amply adequate. God does not reason according to the logic of man; neither are His ways man's ways.

God knew beforehand exactly how He was going to lead Gideon into the promised victory. It would not be by sword, spear, shield, arrows, or armor that they would win this battle. They would never be able to say they had gained the victory by their own prowess with sword and shield. Choosing carefully from His heavenly arsenal of eternal wisdom, Jehovah – the "MIGHTY MAN OF WAR," decided upon these unique weapons for this special occasion – *"The Lord is a man of war; the Lord is His name" (Exodus 15:3)*.

Jehovah chose out for his own right arm his glittering two-edged sword of flaming fire. All the bright heavenly hosts of angels were armed with sharp swords of terrible light to accompany their Commander. God Himself was going to intervene for His people in this brief but glorious moment of Israel's history. He would write a new page for them in the annals of outstanding victories of their glorious nation.

Once more they would behold how their God, Jehovah, miraculously intervened to deliver them from their lamentable captivity. They would know that it was Jehovah and not the gods of the Amorites that gave them such an astonishing victory. And it would also reveal in almost comic contrast, how ridiculously powerless were the Amorite gods. For these gods had no power to save, even when neither sword, spear, nor arrow was raised against them.

By giving His people victory in such a manner, God would bring a revival of worship of Jehovah back to Israel. They would know that Jehovah alone had given them the victory and would turn away from the powerless gods of images of clay and stone. They would surely know those were helpless gods that had no power to help either Israel or even their faithful devotees, the Midianites.

The battle was fought in the season of harvest. Gideon had struggled valiantly all alone in his hidden fields and in the winepress for his own sustenance. Now it was harvest time for all Israel. Everyone would freely gather in a bountiful harvest as they reaped the rich spoil from the Midianites.

This victory was not given only for the benefit of the company of three hundred chosen men. Indeed, they would be enriched in the harvest, but also the whole impoverished, captive, suffering heritage of the Lord would reap a great harvest. God would feed his starving people from the spoil of the armies of three nations. They would have an abundant harvest this year for which they neither plowed, sowed, nor reaped. Empty bins and storehouses would be well filled, for God would provide them with much sustenance from their oppressors – sustenance that had been wickedly plundered and stolen from the Israelites would now be restored in abundance.

25

The Battle Of The Trumpets

The trumpet, a ram's horn, as a weapon? Absolutely... yes! And a very effective one at that when it is wielded by a man of faith. A trumpet becomes a powerful weapon of spiritual warfare when it is used to declare aloud faith's declaration of God's promises. Infinite Wisdom chose the trumpet. He knew the laws of psychological warfare long before Freud invented psychology.

God planned to catch the enemy off guard and waken His sleep-drugged foes with a terrible fright as they peacefully dreamed of rich booty on the morrow. He ordered His little army to erupt their trumpets' voices in harrowing cadence in the ears of the Midianites as they announced their message of doom.

That startling shock would cause the enemy to fantasize the dreadful illusion of hundreds of captains over innumerable companies of warriors attacking them in the darkness. Terrorized into witless combat in the dark night, their frightened imaginations would conjure up before their eyes innumerable thousands of heavily armed Israelites – Israelites that would overrun them and crush them under their feet.

The Commander's Orders

Before the days of electronic communication, it was a common practice in war to use the loud voice of the trumpet to transmit orders to the troops. A trumpeter would stand by his captain and broadcast his orders. Through various trumpet signals and codes, the captain could thereby guide the troops.

An unknown trumpet signal in the dark could easily mislead the enemy into imagining a frightful, fantastic delusion. It would be plausible for the Midianites to think that their whole camp was surrounded by alien troops guided by trumpeters. Naturally, they would assume that they were surrounded by armed Israeli warriors who were full of wrath and vengeance. With terrible Jehovah God helping the Israelites, the Midianites would know they were doomed.

Under such circumstances, it would never occur to the Midianites that it was all a clever ruse designed by Divine Wisdom. Never in the world would they imagine that Gideon's trumpeters were not only signal men, but that they were the whole of the attacking army. A pagan Midianite could never imagine of such audacity of faith in Jehovah as their attackers possessed; it was beyond their powers of comprehension.

Clay Pitchers

When Gideon gave all of his men a large clay pitcher to carry into battle, they looked at one another in astonishment. A big clay pitcher? "What is this for . . . what shall we do with it, Gideon?" they laughed good naturedly. "Shall we bring back our booty in this clay vessel?

"Gideon, how do you expect us to carry this awkward thing noiselessly down into the valley? How can we climb over the rocks and through the thickets on the mountainside and not break it? Don't you know that if just one of us slips, falls, and breaks it, the noise will awaken the whole sleeping army below?" several of his men asked.

"Men," Gideon replied, "these pitchers are to carry lighted torches down to the camp of the enemy. They will hide the torch light from the Midianite sentinels till you arrive at their camp border. At the precise moment I will give this signal; I will smash my pitcher as loudly as I can. You must instantly do the same. At the same moment, we will shout our battle cry of praise unto Jehovah and our faith in the sword of His word."

"We can see your strategy," replied his faithful band. "Blowing the trumpets on every side will doubtlessly bring bewilderment and confusion to the enemy. Then we smash the pitchers while we blow the trumpets. Ah, . . . what a perplexing din and commotion that will make!" they drolly laughed in gleeful anticipation of the deluded disorientation awaiting the enemy. "Gideon, we think you are right – such a noise will frighten them enough to make them too bewildered to fight.

"Incidentally, Gideon, have you considered the fact that the torches will effectively illumine our own faces quite brightly in the darkness? We will become well-lighted targets for their spears and arrows. Also, at the same time, those torches flaming in our own eyes will prevent us seeing beyond them into the darkness."

"Fear not," answered Gideon, "the sudden shock and mind-numbing noise is all God is asking us to do. Remember, we are not depending upon ourselves to win this battle. Our strength is in the strong right arm of our Jehovah.

"Jehovah will greatly amplify that crashing sound in their ears. They will imagine it to be the sound of ten thousand chariots with iron wheels crashing over the stony terrain in an invincible attack. That crashing sound will echo and re-echo from hillside to hillside till they are utterly convinced there is a great army attacking.

"They will hear that crashing sound join our clamorous shouts of praise to Jehovah for victory. Just hearing the Name of Jehovah in our praise alone is enough to frighten them beyond intelligent reaction. They will see the illusion: before their eyes will be a host of valiant warriors rushing towards them in the night with flashing swords, crashing shields, and dashing chariots and horses of war bringing death and destruction to all.

"The Presence of our God is with us; He will fight for us because the battle is the Lord's. My God has shown me that we will not even need sword or shield this night. With no more weapons than these, you shall see the Midianites destroyed. Without any doubt, the slain of the Lord shall be many tonight.

"So friends, carry your pitcher extremely carefully; it is a powerful weapon Jehovah has chosen for us in this battle. He has provided them for us for this hour." Gideon's word of assurance and strong faith lifted high their courage and inspired them to action.

First of all, they needed these pitchers to contain the blazing torches they were to carry into battle. Their torches had to be carried burning and ready. These would be blazing lights confined and covered. Not as much light as the glow of a fire-fly must escape to reveal their approach as they stealthily slipped down the mountainside. Their lighted torches would be absolutely invisible to the enemy sentinels as they silently advanced in the night. These men had to completely conceal their burning torches, yet at the same time, keep them well lighted.

Vessels Of Clay

The clay pitcher typifies the outer human life: the soul, the ego, and the self that conceals the hidden things of the heart. It is the vessel of clay that contains the light and fire of divine life within its covering shell. It typifies the revival of faith brightly burning within the inner heart – well hidden within and not yet made visible to others. Only the soldier himself knew that hidden in his pitcher burned a living faith that had not been there a week before.

For the torch to function as a useful light, the pitcher had to be deliberately broken beyond repair. That breaking of the pitcher symbolized the full surrender of the human life to God. Only then could the burning light within it shine forth in the battle of spiritual life.

This breaking of the clay vessel – that contained the lighted fire – was notoriously reenacted many centuries later. When Mary of Bethany broke the alabaster box of ointment, she thereby liberated its rich perfume. She lavishly poured that ointment upon the feet of Jesus in adoring worship. The breaking of that beautiful alabaster box typified the complete surrender of her self-life. It was like Gideon's three hundred men breaking their pitchers as an act of surrender. It portrayed daring faith as they put their life on the line in obedience to Jehovah.

Breaking the alabaster box of her self-life, Mary allowed the burning light of her adoring heart to illumine all who were present. She chose to break open the restraining coverings of alabaster stone that hid the fire of love in her secret heart. She revealed the treasure of Christ's love brightly burning within. She so desired to manifest the ardent love for Christ within her that she no longer counted her alabaster vessel of value.

The disciples counted Mary's breaking the alabaster box of aromatic ointment and pouring it upon Jesus' feet as a total waste. It made some of them so angry they sharply censured her. "Why all this waste?" they cried. However, Jesus rebuked them because He knew what her actions truly signified. He fully appreciated the loving surrender in her heart. He took her act of devotion, which the disciples considered a waste, and made it a memorial to be treasured and remembered forever unto all future generations. It was then stored in the museum of the history of His saints called the Bible.

Empty Vessels

Obviously, the pitchers of Gideon's band had to be empty. It didn't matter what the pitchers had formerly contained, be it water, milk, or wine. But earthen pitchers definitely could not be used to contain burning torches unless they were empty of anything that would quench the fire within.

"... *Pour out your heart before Him:* ..." *entreated the Psalmist (Psalms 62:8).* There are some believers who are brave and willing to blow the trumpet in the face of the enemy, but they could not tolerate the thought of their pitcher being emptied of the provision of water for the long battle ahead. And most important, they could not bear to break it beyond use or repair even before the battle started.

Half-empty vessels would be useless – for if they were half-full of some other material, they could not contain the lighted torches. A completely empty pitcher was vitally important to God's strategy for this battle. Gideon needed those torches; they must be well-lighted and burning within the empty pitchers to complete the moment of surprise attack. In the crucial moment of the battle that night, those pitchers must be ruthlessly, irremediably broken so the light of the burning torches hidden within might suddenly spring forth.

26

Burning Torches – Wounded Wood?

In Gideon's day torches were made of pieces of naturally resinated wood – wounded wood that took nature many years to grow. A torch was cut from certain kinds of trees that at some prior time were injured and slowly through the years the tree poured healing oils into these wounds. These oils slowly hardened into resin. When the wood became saturated with resin, it was suitable for a brightly burning — a long-lived torch.

These oil-saturated, wounded wooden torches were ready to be set aflame to light Gideon's illustrious battle. Over the years the wounded trees – perhaps trees that were injured long ago when they were just young saplings – found the answer to their hurt. They chose to pour in healing balsam from their roots instead of rotting in the decay of bitterness and resentment. Gradually the trees became saturated with tree-tears from pain that crystallized and permeated every cell, filling each with fragrant balsam oils. The gaping wounds were eased, comforted, and protected by those tears that slowly changed into resin.

Sometimes torch-wood is formed in a more drastic way. When certain trees, such as pine or fir, are cut down the stump remains with its roots intact in the rich soil. The tree then tries to heal its terrible death wound by copiously pouring in great amounts of healing oils. The bit of tree that remains tries to heal itself and ease the pain of the fatal wound that has destroyed its life. After several years the stump becomes permeated with oils and resins oozing out of every cell. What splendid torches can be made from such wood. This is the kind of wood Gideon sought for torches to arm his little army.

Army . . . ? A torch for a weapon . . . ? Truly the ways of the Lord are strange ways. God, as the Creator of man, knows exactly how man functions; He also knows precisely how a man will react to every given stimulus. In His infinite wisdom God chose these weapons to wage psychological warfare. He would exterminate His enemies without using any aggressive cutting weapons of brass or steel. Perhaps this was the only human battle in history that was won by psychological weapons only.

Another Tree, Another Torch, Another Time

Many centuries later God grew a certain tree to make Himself a flaming torch to lighten the darkness of this world in the stupendous battle against the forces of evil. It was the battle that would bring eternal deliverance to His captive people.

In scriptural typology trees symbolize men – earthlings that grow out of the ground. God gave a special name to the tree He chose, "... *And thou shalt call His name Jesus: for He shall save His people from their sins*" *(Matthew 1:21).*

That Tree was mortally wounded, cut off from the ground and died when It was still in Its youth. Not only did It suffer a death wound, but was mutilated and scarred in fearsome manner. So much so that the prophet Isaiah said of It: *"For He shall grow up before Him as a tender plant, and as a root out of a dry ground: . . . He is despised and rejected of men; a Man of sorrows, and acquainted with grief; . . . Surely*

He hath borne our griefs, and carried our sorrows: yet we did esteem Him stricken, smitten of God, and afflicted. But He was wounded for our transgressions, He was bruised for our iniquities: the chastisement of our peace was upon Him; and with His stripes we are healed" (Isaiah 53:2-5).

And there was also another tree that grew in the land of Israel – a tree that was cut down to make for Himself another lighted torch to lighten the darkness. He made His torch from two poles cut from that tree and united them in such a manner that it formed a cross. Then He nailed those two torches together and set them aflame by the fire of His eternal Love.

Another Pitcher To Break

The human body in scripture is called a vessel of clay. There was another Pitcher of very special clay, that Pitcher was named Jesus. He lived as a burning torch of compassion within that Pitcher of clay. His own Father fashioned and exclusively formed that unique pitcher for Him. That Pitcher also, as Gideon's pitcher, had to be broken before the light carried within it could be released. *"That was the true Light which lighteth every man that cometh into the world" (John 1:9). "Wherefore when He cometh into the world, He saith, 'Sacrifice and offering thou wouldest not, but a body hast Thou prepared Me'" (Hebrews 10:5).*

God gave Gideon His strategy and the kind of weapons Gideon would use to begin the revival of true worship and to deliver Israel from His enemies – the strategy and weapons that will ever be useful in restoring revival to His Church. At the same time, God gave Gideon (in type) the picture of world deliverance and world revival that He would bring to pass in the fullness of time – a time when the Messiah would come and on the Cross bring eternal restoration and deliverance from sin and the tyranny of Satan. God used this entire event in the history of Israel to foretell, again through prototype, the story of Jesus and Redemption – showing that through the Sacrifice of Jesus on the Cross and through faith in that Sacrifice, many souls would be delivered from all their enemies.

The story of Gideon is a history exceedingly rich in types and symbols. In symbolic details it depicts the work of Jesus overcoming the satanic enemies of mankind. The pitcher and torch illustrate the Crucifixion, while the trumpet sounds aloud the cry repeated by Martin Luther, **Justification by Faith**. *". . . For by grace are ye saved through faith; and that not of yourselves: it is the gift of God: (Ephesians 2:8).* The details of the entire story are richly portrayed: through the interaction of God and Gideon, by the materials used, through the process of development of God's men, by the ways and means to revival and throughout the battle of deliverance from spiritual oppression.

"Men, Light Your Torches"

Gideon's warriors set their torches aflame on the hilltop; until the wooden torches were burning they were of no use. Unless they were brightly burning, they could give no illumination, nor could they blaze out and lighten the darkness of battle. The long process of preparation of the wood with all its oils was not sufficient – without the fire it still could give no light in the darkness.

God set Gideon aflame when the Angel kindled the fire on the rock and burnt both the wood and his sacrifice. Those same flames entered into Gideon's heart, and he became a torch flaming with revival fires – a torch lighting up the darkness of despair with the bright shining of hope.

"I indeed baptize you with water unto repentance: but He that cometh after me is mightier than I, whose shoes I am not worthy to bear. He shall baptize you with the Holy Ghost, and with fire" (Matthew 3:11). Fire comes down out of Heaven and kindles into brightly burning flames the anointing oil of the Holy Spirit in the resinated wood of human lives. This furnishes the light and power needed in the Christian's battle.

Hidden Beauties

After the torch was kindled, each man was to hide it in the empty pitcher and carry it safely out of sight into the camp of the enemy. The hidden fire of the burning flame lightened and warmed the earthen vessel inside. But the flame-bearing pitcher gave no hint whatsoever to an outside observer of the light and fire it carried within.

The fabulous beauty of the golden jewel of Moses' tabernacle, the Ark of pure gold, was hidden underneath black badger skins. The outside observer could see nothing at all of the hidden beauty within. Inside the dark badger skins of the tabernacle was the light from the fire of the burning golden candlestick. Inside the tabernacle the burning lamp illuminated the incredible cherubim of pure gold and the many jewels of the golden utensils laying beside the altar. Also, inside the tabernacle all the walls were adorned with gorgeous tapestries, woven throughout with threads of gold. All that exquisite beauty was safely hidden from the prying eyes of unconsecrated men under four layers of covering. The outermost covering of the tabernacle was the most unattractive of all, black badger skins.

The precious things of God are always hidden from carnal eyes of mere curiosity. The precious things of earth are well hidden and must be diligently sought after. Gold or diamonds, pearls or petroleum are all stashed away in their hiding places. So also, the precious things of the celestial world that exist on earth are made to be much more invisible to the unbelieving eye. They are well hidden in their covering of clay until the moment of revelation comes. *"Beloved, now are we the sons of God, and it doth not yet appear what we shall be: but we know that, when He shall appear, we shall be like Him; for we shall see Him as He is"* (1 John 3:2).

Pitchers Must Be Broken

The inside of a pitcher is a decidedly unfriendly environment in which to maintain a burning fire; the flame would have to be carefully nurtured in some ingenious way with a constant flow of oxygen. How easily the flame could fade and die. Just a little carelessness, a little lack of attention and the flame within would have been smothered into darkness.

To release the light to shine effectively in the darkness, it was necessary to break the pitcher. The fire remained completely hidden within and only a clay pitcher was visible until it was deliberately destroyed. Each soldier had to voluntarily demolish his pitcher at the given moment before the light contained within could be released to illuminate the battle in the black night.

The vessel of clay safely concealed the light and fire abiding within so the little army could remain protected in darkness. Their surprise attack remained securely sheltered in the opaque mantle of night. The pitchers faithfully hid their blazing light until the appointed time.

The intrepid three hundred slipped carefully, silently down the steep hillside. No ray of light exposed the threat of coming destruction to the sleeping Midianites. Even though they had been fairly warned by Gideon's trumpet, the enemy incredulously slumbered carelessly in the darkness. They trusted, but vainly, in the security of their vast military strength. They were totally unaware that they were being surrounded by a small band of committed men with burning firebrands of vengeance in their hands.

Those torches in the clay pitchers did not illuminate the soldier's way down the dark mountainside. Those bright torches could not be used to help them descend into the valley of battle. In the darkness of night, they had to carefully feel their way down the wild unmarked terrain with only the dim light from the stars to help them.

Their carefully nurtured fire and light must wait till the strategic moment indicated by the Heavenly Commander. Then, they all as one man would smash those pitchers beyond repair with one hard deliberate blow. Immediately, the liberated light from the hidden torches would appear in the eyes of the enemy as the consuming fires of Sheol on the day of judgment.

How faithfully this action portrays the experience of those believers who are numbered in the band of the three hundred valiant ones – those who love not their lives unto death. Ere the inner light can shine forth, there must be a smashing death-blow to the vessel of clay – the *human ego* and the *self-life*.

Some are willing to walk a life of obedience as prescribed by a given standard of living, but they stoutly maintain one condition – "Let me live. Let me remain in control. Leave my life and lifestyle intact. I will serve, but in my own way, my own time, and with my own conditions." It is the rebel cry of self – the ruling potentate within.

Prepared Weapons

Neither the torches, the pitchers, nor the trumpets God ordered were prepared by some cheap, quick, overnight process. Weapons for the valiant ones, marching with their Commander into the war of deliverance, were especially prepared and carefully formed. To make weapons that are true, faithful, and effective, God may use methods of preparation that are even painful and difficult.

The trumpets were made from the horns of aged rams, horns that had grown long and sonorous. It required the long life of a ram to produce a graceful, useful horn that could become a trumpet. Furthermore, the horns could only be harvested at the death of the ram. So once again, death was required to provide the instrument God so powerfully used as a weapon in the hands of Gideon.

However, in its natural state a ram's horn was not useful as a trumpet. Only a certain kind of ram had the right material in its horn to make a trumpet. From those selected rams, they had to find horns that had just the right shape and curvature. After harvesting the horns, they had to polish them till all uneven bumps and swellings were removed. Finally, they had to cut the tips just right and mold them into proper mouthpieces to be able to produce the right sound.

The pitchers began their existence as raw clay dug from special quarries. Then the clay was laboriously cleaned from all debris, washed free from all contaminants, molded into pitchers and baked in the hot kiln in the potter's house. Only after a long and strenuous process, could a bit of raw clay become a pitcher useful to carry the torch. And then it had to be broken to release the light that was carried within it.

Triumphant trumpets, prepared pitchers, and tortured torches were unique instruments distinctively prepared by

God. God provided three hundred of each of these distinctive weapons and gave them to Gideon for his dedicated band there on the hilltop by the well of Harod.

With discerning insight God chose these men. There was not one among them who would rebelliously determine to go into battle carrying refreshing water in his pitcher instead of a kindled torch. Not one would dispute with the commander and say, "We need the waters for refreshment in the heat of the battle." God had already sifted such men out of His army.

Some people think that deliverance from captivity can only be won by loud shouting, fierce struggling, and strong arms of mighty warriors using fierce weapons in the war. But when the dust of such a battle settles, it is only to discover the dreadful consequences of that unleashed violence. If Gideon had insisted on fighting that battle in the usual manner, it would have resulted in total defeat for his army and victory for the Midianites. The Israelites would have continued hiding in their caves of captivity. Perhaps a very few wounded warriors might have escaped to some dark den to nurse their battle wounds and rue the day of battle. This would have been the story, if Gideon's men had followed man's rationale instead of following the wisdom of God in His ordained ways.

This was not an ordinary skirmish, but a life and death battle ordered by God. Those Midianites were not ordinary enemies but three nations of vicious oppressors that hated Israel. Therefore, God did not bring against them ordinary arms of warfare, but He used extraordinary weapons of might and power. The Midianites would find as their antagonists a carefully selected army with very special arms and Almighty Jehovah – Israel's living God – accompanying them.

God's carefully selected army is:

... Gideon's three hundred with trumpets, pitchers and torches;

... David facing Goliath with sling and stone;

... thirty valiant men of David's royal guard;

... seventy royal guards accompanying Solomon's chariot;

... Samson with the jawbone of an ass;

... Joel's unconquerable army marching through the land;

... Paul victorious in the arena of wild beasts at Ephesus;

... Perfect Submission nailed to a tree;

... Jesus Triumphant beside an empty tomb.

🔥 **27** 🔥

"Look On Me"

"And he said unto them, 'Look on me, and do likewise: and, behold, when I come to the outside of the camp, it shall be that, as I do, so shall ye do'" (Judges 7:17).

"Look on me." What a strange order to give to men who were enfolded in the opaque blanket of the dark night. "When you have found your place, surrounded the encampment, and are all ready, then direct your eyes to yonder willows. I will already be there with my company. Carefully observe me and imitate at once everything I do – in that way we shall act completely in unison as one man," Gideon succinctly ordered his valiant men.

Each warrior would be separated from his fellow by many yards of darkness and deep shadows when the three hundred men finally surrounded the enemy's camp on all three sides. Therefore, they would find it effectually impossible to see one another in the moonless starlight. How then would it be possible to see their commander across the encampment several hundred yards distant? Furthermore, impediments of all kinds would interfere with their vision: tents, shrubs, boulders, asses, horses, or camels could stand in their line of sight.

How could their commander possibly expect them to look on him, see what he did and then immediately imitate his actions? Their eyes were not made for night vision. Perhaps the eyes of a cat or an owl can see their prey in the dim light of the midnight stars, but these were ordinary Hebrew farmers. Nevertheless, Gideon ordered them to watch and imitate him there in the darkness. And not one man presumed to question the possibility of obeying Gideon or how to do it. They received his orders and determined to implicitly obey.

Light In Their Darkness

Was their obedience to this unique command yet another miracle in that night of miracles? The scribe of the Book of Judges failed to explain how they accomplished this feat. Did the three hundred have some kind of prophetic insight to lighten their eyes? Or were they somehow so harmonized with their commander – so attuned to his spirit and so at one with his battle strategy – that they could intuitively **see** him even though all were covered with a deep mantle of starlit shadows? One thing is certain, Gideon's band fulfilled that order, but how they were able to do it remains a mystery.

However they worked it out, it remains a fact of history that as men of God – with their eyes fixed upon their commander – they were able to see him and obediently replicate his actions. In spite of the adverse circumstances and the many hindering obstructions, they looked to their captain with a **single eye** that . . . **filled their whole body with light.** *"The light of the body is the eye: If therefore thine eye be single, thy whole body shall be full of light" (Matthew 6:22).*

Men who can see well enough in the dim starlight to pull down and destroy the idols in their own backyards will have no problem keeping their eye on their Commander while all around darkness reigns. Such men are lighted ones – followers of their Commander that have light within themselves amidst the darkness of this world. They can walk without falling in the rough terrain of the battlefield. They are those who keep their eyes firmly fixed upon their Leader as He leads them forth into victory.

"Do As I Do"

Only by carefully keeping their commander in sight could the three hundred receive their orders and be able to do the right thing at the right moment. The secret of their success lay in their sudden terrorizing surprise attack. Therefore, Gideon could not possibly be shouting out orders in that moment.

However, success also lay in their acting in unison to present a valid ruse of a solid frontal attack. Therefore, Gideon's men could not do their own thing, one at a time in their own time. Timing was essential; disunity or acting in an unsynchronized manner as free undisciplined spirits would jeopardize the whole plan. They were too few to attack in a wild, helter-skelter, haphazard fashion; such action would totally invalidate Gideon's astute strategy.

The conclusive battle, that would destroy forever the Midianite yoke over Israel, could not be won by independent-minded men each running his own show. "Lone Rangers" do not fit well in God's army. The command was to follow the leader and keep under orders; there were no alternate orders. Silence must reign absolute till the crucial instant; then, that silence would be fiercely fractured with the soul-shattering clamor of trumpets and crashing din of smashed pitchers.

The order, "Do as I do," thoroughly abrogated the principle of *"each man doing what was right in his own eyes."*

Later that principle came into vogue in Israel. *"In those days there was no king in Israel: every man did that which was right in his own eyes" (Judges 21:25).*

This was the battle of the Lord – Jehovah Himself had given the battle plan, established its strategy, and ordered its action. He had called, prepared and set His captain into place. Jehovah, not Gideon, had sifted and chosen His army for this battle. He also had seen to it that the men of His choice had the *spirit of obedience* in their hearts. He knew that they would follow their leader without question or hesitation in absolute obedience. And He had specifically chosen their weapons – the most unique arms a soldier ever bore.

"I Do What He Does"

Jesus said, *"I do what I see the Father do; I speak what I hear My Father speak" (John 5:19 and 8:28 paraphrased).* In the stygian darkness of this world Jesus was able to see His Father at all times. Neither impeding circumstance, nor the fierce forces of hell's own darkness could hide His Father's face from Him. To Him the gloomy darkness of this outer world shone with the bright light of noon lighted by the rays of celestial light flowing from their mutual infinite love.

The earthly Gideon of long ago, who was a type of Christ, expected his followers to keep their eyes fastened upon him. *"Wherefore seeing we also are compassed about with so great a cloud of witnesses, let us lay aside every weight, and the sin which doth so easily beset us, and let us run with patience the race that is set before us, looking unto Jesus the author and finisher of our faith; who for the joy that was set before Him endured the Cross, despising the shame, and is set down at the right hand of the Throne of God" (Hebrews 12:1-2).*

Captain Jesus also expects His followers to faithfully keep their eyes upon Him in their crucial battle of faith while darkness reigns in the night of this world. Not only are the eyes of His warriors to be fixed exclusively upon their Captain, but their actions are to be identical to His actions – they are under orders to *"do as He does."*

God does not give His followers license to follow the carnal mind and invent ingenious schemes of their own inspiration in the battle of deliverance from evil. Man working alone – not carefully guided by his Leader – cannot overcome the adversary. The follower of Jesus must follow specific orders – orders that He will give step-by-step as the battle progresses. Whatever followers see their Leader do, they must also do.

The three hundred's strict military orders from their commander left no room for personal interpretations; after all they were locked into a battle of survival. Their life was on the line. It was a case of winner takes all. There was no provision for defeat. Their lives, their families, and their future all depended on winning; there was no such thing as a half-win situation.

Israel was already a conquered people – vassals under servitude to the Midianites. They did not start the war, but they determined to both end the war and their vassalage. They all knew that there was only one road to victory. Totally out-powered and out-numbered, they had not the luxury of individual choice. They would follow their leader's orders implicitly or be destroyed.

"Go Down From This Mountain"

Leaving the security of their mountaintop and the place of safety where the refreshing waters flowed from Harod's well, Gideon and his men, as quiet as the shadow of the hunting fox, vacated their camp, and crept down to the borders of the enemy's armies. Down into the darkness of the enemy infested valley the valiant three hundred slipped silently.

They knew well where they were going, why they were going and the risks they were taking by going there. However, the gloom of sinister shades in the valley or fears of defeat did not disturb or delay their going. Over rocks and around trees they carefully crept down the mountain into the valley. These men, who had survived for seven years by stalking the deer in the night, had learned how to creep over the terrain so silently that the keen ear of the deer would not register alarm.

Ever keeping a wary eye on the bright star overhead, as it slowly closed the distance to the high rock on the hilltop, they painstakingly carried their precious pitchers and nursed their burning treasure within. Not a foot slipped; not a loose rock dislodged to roll down the hill. They reached the valley floor without mishap; not one sentinel was alerted. They breathed praises to God for His mercies.

It was well past midnight when they all reached the valley floor and dispersed themselves around the enemy's camp. Their guiding star had given them enough time ere it set behind the western mountain peak; they had still a few minutes to spare. Quietly and stealthily each man found his own place and waited poised for action.

Gideon had given the order, *"When I blow with a trumpet, I and all that are with me, then blow ye the trumpets also on every side of all the camp, and say, 'The sword of the Lord, and of Gideon'" (Judges 7:18)*. Gideon and his company would defiantly sound forth their challenge by the ringing voice of the trumpets.

Listening ears, if they were well tuned, would be able to hear the echoing challenge of Michael's trumpet thundering out from the heavenlies, adding its triumphant voice to their victor cry. Gideon fully expected the heavenly host to join them and to blow their celestial trumpets without delay – sounding forth the divine challenge. Gideon's trumpet, Michael's trumpet, angel trumpets, and the trumpets of the three hundred would join in one mighty voice declaring the devastating message, "BY THE SWORD OF THE LORD GOD AND OF GIDEON, HIS CHOSEN COMMANDER, WE TAKE VENGEANCE UPON YOU MIDIANITES."

28

"Attack, Attack, Attack!"

The guiding star by which they synchronized their attack finally reached the top of the out-cropping on the hilltop. Suddenly the calm stillness of the night exploded into a cacophony of lethal clamor; three hundred trumpets reverberated in unison. At the same moment three hundred voices burst into a thunderous battle cry that echoed and reechoed from hillside to hillside. The sleepy quietness that reigned was shattered beyond recovery. Death prevailed in every audible vibration.

Gideon's trumpet authoritatively sounded out attack orders to the invisible troops, and in the same instant, three hundred more blaring trumpets amplified the same command. Each trumpeter jubilantly played a triumphant note of positive faith in God in exultant melody, urging onward their innumerable invisible troops. To the astounded ears of the sleeping Midianites, the terrible sound was multiplied ten thousand times as it continued to echo across the valley.

Then the chief war Angel sent to fight with them, blew His trumpet and His accompanying hosts did the same; the inaudible sound penetrated straight into the enemies' dazed brains erasing any wits they might of had left. The Midianite army knew not which way to turn or on which side to fight. Paralyzing panic seized control of their still half-somnambulant members.

This tempestuous tumult triggered chaotic actions of confusion and catastrophic discord in the aroused camp of the enemy. When the ordered sound of battle blasted into the ears of the slumbering Midianites, they had not the slightest clue of how many men were in the ambush.

Hard upon the frightening blasts of the trumpets and the terrorizing shouts of mighty faith, there came yet further terrorizing sound. An explosive detonation blasted through the night air into the enemy's tortured ears. Gideon had struck a sharp shattering blow to his pitcher that was immediately multiplied by three hundred more shattering blows fracturing the night air.

The terrifying sounds of destruction surrounded the enemy in the darkness like a howling tornado; it was the merciless whirlwind of Gideon's barley cake. From every point of the compass came the sharp sudden din of smashing shards. Just as Gideon had anticipated, to the bewildered ears of the baffled Midianites, it sounded like the clashing of steel on steel. It reverberated like ten thousand chariots of iron careening over the valley floor – their wheels smashing into the rocks as they dashed into the fray.

Simultaneously, accompanying those terrifying sounds of shattered shards, blazing torches suddenly leaped into high flame and sent their bewildering light into the stygian darkness of their reeling minds. In the eyes of the Midianites, that disorienting light seemed to show every face they illuminated as faces of bitter enemies contorted with the wrath of vengeance. In every direction they turned, they faced bright blazing torches illuminating the faces of mighty warriors pouncing upon them as a whole pride of lions charging one lone perplexed hare.

Judgment Hour

The sound of shattering shards that slivered the air struck the hour of vengeance on the clock of God. God's time of judgment had arrived for the Jehovah-hating, murderous Midianites. Until that hour, the Midianites had believed they could destroy Jehovah's heritage with impunity. But the patience of God had ended; just retribution was to be measured out to them suddenly and without quarter. The hour had arrived when Divine Justice chose to demand an accounting for all their merciless cruelties and ruthless persecution of His people.

It also was the hour of divine liberation for all the suffering vassals of the Midianites. The fire and light that had been well hidden in the darkness within earthen vessels sprang forth to announce the dawning sunrise of a new day in Israel.

Confusion

While those earthen pitchers remained whole in the darkness they were no threat at all to the enemy. But when broken and cast onto the ground in unrecoverable shards, the very sound of their breaking brought consternation to the enemy. The liberated fire-light brought lethal disorientation.

The attack fulfilled precisely what God previously revealed to Gideon. The wild sounds of violent war caused their enemies' contorted imaginations to conjure up before their eyes hundreds of captains ordering countless thousands of Israeli warriors into battle.

What utter confusion! What an awful revelation! The light of the knowledge of the hour of inexorable judgment seized the Midianites. The inexplicable mystery of those blazing torches blinded and confused them. That flaming light made the wrathful faces of the valiant avengers appear as terrible specters before their terrified eyes. The faces of the three hundred were transfigured by their torches into flaming invincible messengers of Divine Justice.

With torches held high, the three hundred beheld the deadly confusion and chaos that engulfed the ranks of the three enemy nations. In their panic stricken state, every enemy warrior believed his neighbor to be an intruding Israelite. Their minds were so deathly frightened that – in spite of the light of those torches – not one of the enemy could recognize a friend. Each warrior perceived his neighbor as a foe to be feared and slain.

Jehovah Is With Them

As the valiant band shouted their mighty battle cry of faith, "BY THE SWORD OF JEHOVAH AND OF GIDEON," its message reverberated from every side in the terrible darkness. Uninhibited confusion confiscated control over the frightened army with the speed of sound. The mention of God's Divine Name imparted yet greater terror in the ears of the enemy. Those words carried the sentence of death to the Midianites. With the suddenness of an earthquake, they knew with awful certainty that their day of reckoning had come and there was no escape.

They had already heard too much about mighty Jehovah and feared Him terribly. They did not know just how He would fight against them. Would He slay them as He did the Egyptians? Send hosts of choleric angels against them? Hurl down hail and fiery darts with pursuing thunder upon their heads? However He would fight, the terrified Midianites knew beyond any doubt they were doomed to utter destruction. In conscience stricken terror they lashed out desperately, mindlessly against whatever or whoever was around them.

God answered the faith of His little band by sending His terrible flaming swords above and around the Midianite army. Flashing furiously in the darkness before their frightened and confused eyes, swords, two-edged and fiery, flashed and slashed in the gloomy shadows – swords wielded by mighty angels sent to wreak vengeance upon the frightened armies. Dreadful rays from the fiery swords of the angelic host shot unimpeded into their terrorized brains burning out all powers of logic and reason. What little courage might have remained fled precipitously from their hearts.

All trust and confidence in their own motley ranks of hirelings and mercenaries were transformed into fear and hate. All their faith in their dumb idols vanished precipitately into the dark pit of oblivion when the name of Jehovah rang out in the night air. Reverberations of the battle cry, "BY THE SWORD OF JEHOVAH AND OF GIDEON," like red hot points of steel, engraved the lethal realization upon their crazed brains that mighty Jehovah was fighting for Israel – death was in His hands.

Every Man Against His Fellow

"And the three hundred blew the trumpets, and the Lord set every man's sword against his fellow, even throughout all the host: . . ." (Judges 7:22).

Suddenly, unexplainably their terrible, blood-thirsty swords they had long used against Israel, were now turned in wrath against themselves. The cruel, sharp blades they had artfully wielded to bring discord, confusion, and strife, now brought death to themselves. They felt the cold terrible steel in their own vitals. Sadly they discovered by experience how deadly and destructive their swords were. Because Jehovah turned those steel blades upon their own bodies as they swung them in confusion and suspicion, they slashed out the life-blood one from the other.

The confusion of the Midianites and their Amalakite helpers was sudden and terrible. The frightening screams of agony and the terrible groans of the dying intensified their mortal dread and panic. Their senses were addled, their eyes blinded, and their instincts dulled. The enemy nations that had lifted up their swords against Jehovah's people were now smitten by their own weapons. Midianite slew Midianite, confederate killed confederate, and fellow turned against fellow. Every man's sword was turned against his own companions.

Friend arose against friend; ally thrust his sword into ally. Midianite, Amalakite, and Ishmaelite each fought against the other. In their disoriented uproar, every neighbor became a deadly enemy to be slain. There was no one to deliver; each man stood undefended and alone. Every man appeared to be a foe to be feared and slaughtered. Like tigers corralled – like crazed mad-men – they furiously sought to slay one another.

Meanwhile, Gideon and his men stood inexorably immovable shouting forth their battle cry, *"The sword of the Lord and of Gideon,"* while continuously trumpeting out their battle orders unto the invisible hosts they were directing.

Too Late

Many decades before, there was a time in history when the Midianites worshiped Jehovah. Moses' father-in-law was a priest of Midian and was well acquainted with Jehovah and His marvelous power and works. In fact, their forefather Midian was a son of Abraham by his second wife Keturah. But they had turned away from God into the depths of idolatry. They chose the idols and religion of the Canaanites in place of Jehovah. They had warred against Jehovah's people, and after defeating them, they had viciously persecuted them.

"Why did we leave Jehovah? Why did we deliberately torment His people?" many a blood-stained warrior asked himself as he lay dying of his wounds on the battlefield. "We feared this might happen. We knew that it is always dangerous and foolish to hurt the people of Jehovah. No one who has ever persecuted the Hebrews has ever prospered for long; retribution is horrible. We are doomed, and it is all our own fault. Why did we not leave well enough alone? Now we shall die in our sins; we are lost and damned." Too late they listened to the voice of conscience accusing them for their heinous acts of hatred and rapine.

The Battle Is The Lord's

God had said He would fight for Israel, yet He deigned not to stain His sword with blood. He turned every man's sword against his neighbor. There was no escape in any direction for the enemy was utterly bewildered and deceived. Without forewarning they were thrown precipitously into utter disaster.

Gideon's men shared in the scenes and the glory of the triumph of God's mighty victory. They were privileged to watch – to see with their eyes and hear with their ears – the mighty intervention of their God. He permitted them to share with Him in His hour of triumph. He allowed them to march with Him and to be workers "together with Him." However, their part was not to slay, kill, nor stain their swords with blood. Their part in the battle was to:

... stand firm,

... praise with the trumpets,

... shout in faith their battle cry of victory,

... keep their torches burning,

... break their earthen pitchers and then see the mighty hand of Jehovah God at work.

The work, the battle, and the victory were God's. Gideon's men were not at all mistaken in this. They knew that the powerful intervention they had seen was of the Lord – not of themselves. They only stood and waited until the expected promises were fulfilled. Their enemies ran about in chaotic confusion; they shouted lies, and cried out vengeance and challenge. Then suddenly, the terrible unseen hosts of Heaven stepped into the midst of the battle and confounded the minds of the enemy till they thought every companion a deadly foe.

"Having Done All, Stand"

Gideon and his men did not run into the midst of the enemy host and try to help God. They stood firm, immoveable, faithful witnesses of the marvelous victory of the Lord and of His Christ. It was the mighty invincible sword of Jehovah in which they trusted and rested. That was enough; they needed no more.

What victorious faith they found in their Jehovah, God of Israel. These were not God's little helpers running around and getting in His way. These were God's chosen men who knew how to obey and stand in their appointed place trusting in the arm of the Lord. They knew that they were not going to get the victory themselves and become little heroes. They knew how to wait on the Lord. They had entered into rest and had ceased from their own labors. God had said, "I will deliver them into your hands." They believed His immutable word. Victory lay in their obedience, even in the face of great danger when every order was contrary to logic and human reasoning.

They Stood In Place

The screaming enemy cried out his challenge to one and all while dashing here and there with flashing steel meting out death on every side to one another. But the valiant avengers only stood and watched the battle of the Lord. Gideon's men stood rock firm – planted as immovable as the hills behind them; each one stood in his own place. They surrounded the enemy and remained an impassable barrier binding them in on all sides; yet they were untouchable behind the shield of the Lord.

Let the enemy challenge and cry out his plans of vengeance; each man stood immovably firm in his place. Let the adversary brandish sword or sharpened spear; Gideon's men stood like a rock. Let the enemy cry and panic. Let the whole camp scream out invocations for succor from gods, rulers, and highest principalities. The three hundred still stood resolute, unyielding.

That was real faith – faith in action, faith that stood victoriously against all the enemy could do. They yielded not a single step to the enemy, as they waited upon their God to work His promised victory. So believing, they waited and stood still, each man in his own place.

Nevertheless, each one ceased not to blow his frightening trumpet giving orders to their invisible army. Those trumpeting voices pounded powerful premonitions into the fear saturated ears of the enemy. The sound of the trumpet continually reminded the Lord God of Israel that the hour of battle was not yet over, and continually called into Heaven for His divine intervention. Their victorious voices shouted aloud their triumphant battle cry; they announced the hour of Israel's deliverance and the utter termination of their slavery.

Victory

The glorious dawn of Israel's long awaited day of deliverance broke over the land as bloodied night gave place to golden dawn. God had come in answer to their cries and set His people free. The enemy's days of cruel mastery over God's heritage suddenly terminated with terrible mortal finality without remedy.

Slowly, the din of battle subsided. Gradually the screams and groans of dissolution grew silent. Countless thousands of slain warriors set out on their journey of no return. They were on their way to meet their Maker and Judge. The clash and clang of steel on steel was heard no more. The enemy lay in heaps and mounds – slain by their own swords. Only those that managed to slip through the gaps between the trumpeters escaped with their lives and ran ignominiously into the night.

All was still in the valley of Jezreel. The trumpets sounded no longer; the glorious battle was over. The only sound heard that early morning was the sweet melodious song of praise unto Jehovah from the unwounded three hundred. They rejoiced and marveled at the miracle and at the God of miracles. Their wonderful Jehovah had magnificently fulfilled His promises and delivered them from all their enemies.

29

Victory

Faith that dares to believe God together with implicit obedience to His commands is an invincible combination of virtues. Faith and obedience release powerful forces of deliverance and provide a wide open door through which God may send the Spirit of revival to liberate the captives. Gideon believed God and fearlessly and fully obeyed the orders spoken to him, even to the point of laying his life on the line. His faith and that obedience were gloriously rewarded by Jehovah Shalom, abundantly fulfilling His promise.

Immeasurable joy filled the hearts of Gideon's battle companions as they saw Jehovah fight for them in that short, sharp battle. At long last the intolerable years of captivity were over; the year of release had come. It was truly a year of Jubilee. Cold cruel winter gave place to reviving spring. Hunger and fasting would become feast and plenty. Jehovah's strong right arm, mighty to save, had brought them the victory. They felt as free as birds escaped from the fowler – as safe as a hound-pursued hart that found the waterbrook.

They Sang A New Song

The trumpeters changed their tune and proclaimed the melody of victory in jubilant voice. Sending their message of success over hill and valley, they trumpeted in clarion voice:

"Hear, O Israeli ears, Jehovah has returned to us and given us the victory!

"The mighty Midianites are fallen; behold they lay in heaps and mounds.

"They are defeated; they are dead; they shall never rise again to torment us.

"Their gods failed them utterly. Baal could not help them.

"Mighty Baal is fallen; he fell with the slain when he heard the ineffable name of Jehovah.

"Jehovah, the Almighty God of Israel, lives forever and reigns over the nations.

"He vanquished all the hosts of Midian and Edom; He triumphed over them without sword, spear, or shield.

"With a broken pitcher, a lively trumpet, and a burning torch, He put to shame the cold steel of lance and sword.

"The Midianites boasted themselves in Baal; they called on his name in the battle; in the cold terror of the night they cried to him; but he heard them not! Baal had fallen and was helpless in the midst of them.

"Jehovah Shalom unsheathed His sword of light, and the enemy fell ignominiously in the darkness for they had no light.

"God sent His Angel of death over their hosts in the frightening night – like the time He delivered our fathers from the tyranny of Egypt.

"Rejoice, for our Redeemer has redeemed us from the tormenting tyrant.

"The feast of the Sabbath year is set before us; come to the feast for there is a bountiful supply.

"Jehovah has spread a table before us here in the valley of Jezreel. Come one; come all. Come and dine for there is booty and rations to spare."

The wonder of their deliverance was heralded by three hundred trumpets when the battle ended – even as the victors pursued the few Midianites that managed to escape for awhile. Rapturously lilting over the hills of Manasseh, from the great sea to the Jordan River, the joyous tidings sped. With great euphoria they proclaimed the thrilling news, *"The Lord has given us the victory!* His mighty arm and His fiery sword have set us free from famine and cruelty. He has trampled our enemies under His feet."

The faith of Gideon and his band was magnificently rewarded by their gracious Jehovah. He sent revival and delivered His people, His choice inheritance, and His beloved Church. Again divine grace broke the chains of captivity and its poignant pangs of poverty and misery.

"Spread The Tidings O'er Hill And Valley"

The dancing rays of the morning light quickened the glad news to the pessimistic citizens as they sat dolefully expecting the sad news of defeat and the death of their fine young valiant sons. But hear, . . . hear all unbelieving ones, the watchers from the hilltop are shouting across the valleys, "Victory, our God has given us the victory! Our God has saved us; we are free! This is the day to rejoice and be glad. Revival has come! The Spirit of Jehovah is with us again."

Joyous women carried the glad tidings from house to house. Excited children ran screeching from cave to cave. Sturdy youths hurriedly climbed the hills from hold to hold, while others spread the wondrous tidings from town to town.

"Our God has given us the victory! The Midianites are defeated! Their mighty army is destroyed! We are free!" The welcome words winged joyously from Israelite to Israelite in cheerful repetition.

"Gideon and his three hundred have prevailed. As the sun overcomes the darkest night, so our God has triumphed over the proud Midianites and their allies. They are vanquished. Their haughty warriors lie heaped in the valley floor as a great heap of rubbish. There they lie – a great feast of flesh for the birds and carrion eaters.

"That arrogant nation has been humbled by the sword of the Lord and of Gideon. In the shame of their defeat they will feel the bitter bite of impoverishment in their own bellies. The time of their brutal tyranny over us is ended; sudden destruction has come upon them without remedy for there is none to help."

The Lord Is God

"Jehovah has returned in mercy and set us free. The Lion of the Tribe of Judah scattered the vaunted Midianites as if they were a herd of deer. He turned again in great mercy and mighty power. He graciously pardoned our iniquities and forgave our sins. He has turned our shameful sorrow into joy, our humiliation into glory and our captivity into liberty. Jehovah is His name – the God of Abraham, Isaac, Jacob, Moses, and Joshua. Once again He has become our God – the God of Gideon. Let His praises sound forth from every hill and valley. Let thanksgiving arise unto Heaven from every heart. God is great and greatly to be praised.

"Behold, it is true!" ever increasingly rang out the glad cry as town and village picked up the wondrous news. "We are the heritage of Jehovah – the God of Israel. We truly are His chosen people. He has not abandoned us and turned His face away from us. We no longer shall be the followers of the gods of the Amorites. After all our painful sacrifices to Baal, still he did not help us. And Moloch, who devoured our children, lifted not a finger of succor. As for that goddess Ashtaroth, her lusts proved but a vain shadow for hope. See and take notice – those gods could not even defend the Midianites, their own devotees; when our Jehovah came to help us, they became helpless and undefended, as a flock of shepherdless sheep before a pack of hungry wolves.

"Jehovah is the true God. Jehovah is the mighty God. We will serve Him and offer our sacrifices unto Him. Let us throw down the altars to their false idols, for gods they are not. They have no power to hurt us; behold, our fear was in vain. We shall do like Gideon and throw down those dumb idols and build an altar to Jehovah. Let us all put Baal away and return unto our God for He has helped us mightily and delivered us from our enemies. Even though we offended Him, yet He is ever merciful and has pardoned us and delivered us from our dreadful oppression.

"Baal and his minions are liars. Where were their vaunted powers of which their priests boasted? They said Baal is more powerful than Jehovah. Behold how miserably those gods failed in the face of mighty Jehovah. The enemy threatened, they boasted, they rested in the security of the power of Baal. Like vain Lilliputians they lifted themselves up against our God. Behold, O daughters of Israel – laugh, . . . dance, . . . sing and shake your heads in derision. The Midianites with their gods are fallen like stones into the sea of despair. In mortal shame and eternal humiliation they have fallen – forever vanquished by the power of our God."

And as the news spread, the glory and wonder of it seized every Hebrew heart and set their feet to dancing and their hearts to singing.

The Midianites' demon-gods ignominiously fled back to the nether regions from whence they came; discordantly routed and abjectly defeated, they tumbled headlong back into the pit. Almighty Jehovah blew His breath upon them and their hearts melted. His terrible thunders discomfited them. He laughed at their arrogant boasting. He sent forth His terrible flaming sword; like mighty lightning thrusts it pierced them through and through.

"Hear, O Israel: The Lord our God is one Lord" (Deuteronomy 6:4). He only is the one true God. Jehovah Shalom is His name.

This Is The Day

What a day of gladness and joy! Like hares from their burrows, Hebrews bounded forth from their hiding places with joyful acclamations. From their dank dens and comfortless caves, they poured out as scattered sheep responding to the call of the shepherd at feeding time. Streams of impoverished humanity came streaming across the hills. They came to the hilltop at the well of Harod and gazed in amazed wonder into the valley below. There lay heaps and piles of mutilated corpses – the remains of a once proud host of three nations. Israel's Jehovah, with but a handful of valiant Israelites, had destroyed forever their oppressive power. There the enemy lay, with all their stolen possessions, forever abandoned into the hands of the victors.

It was a *day of joy, . . . a day of singing, . . . a day of jubilee, . . . a day of mirth and gladness.* The people brought forth their harps and cymbals; young and old danced and praised God in joyful ecstasy and thanksgiving. Once again hope and peace found lodging in their hearts.

That glad day Israel sang anew:

. . . songs of Gideon and his intrepid three hundred,

. . . songs of the flashing fiery two-edged sword of the Lord,

. . . songs of Gideon's Angel and the numberless hosts of the Lord who fought for Israel,

. . . songs of derision of the Midianites and their gods.

In raptures of joy the redeemed held a feast of praise and thanksgiving, as they gathered to the table Jehovah had spread for them in the valley.

Decreed by Moses, every seventh year was a year of rest. It was always ushered in by heralding trumpets. Now again the trumpeters were playing the pleasing melody. The lyrics of a bountiful feast from the abandoned Midianite camp promised a welcome relief to the hungry and starving Hebrews.

For seven years Israel had been ground under the heel of their oppressors – suffering pillage, hunger, pain, fear, and death from their merciless hand. But now the Sabbath of the seventh year had come. It was ushered in that day by three hundred singing trumpets. Starving, impoverished Israel entered into a time of peace and rest. A time they had long craved and prayed for; they thought it would never come. Jehovah Shalom, their ancient and true God, had answered their cries, destroyed their oppressors and given them peace.

30

His Name Is Gideon

In Hebrew the name Gideon means *"one who cuts down or destroys";* therefore, by extension the word means *a warrior* – one who cuts down and destroys his enemies. Many Old Testament personalities are figures that represent Christ in various aspects of His life and works. Gideon, in this extraordinary battle of Israel's history, quite aptly represents Jesus in His redemptive battle to deliver His people from their vassalage to sin.

Many centuries after the deliverance of Gideon, Jesus came into this world as another Warrior – another Gideon. The weapons that Gideon and his three hundred used were a figure of the weapons Christ would use to win the supreme triumph over the arch-enemies of mankind. No other military victory ever won in the history of the world could equal the glorious triumph of Jesus the Conqueror – Jesus, the Gideon who cut down and destroyed the demonic enemies of man.

He triumphed over the devil, the relentless deceiver and adversary, and his hosts of demons. He overcame death, the universal destroyer that eventually swallows every descendant of Adam and Eve in his insatiable maw. He destroyed the power of sin so it no longer held the right of dominion over all flesh. No man, no conqueror, nor any army of mankind had ever overthrown the nemesis of all flesh – sin. Jesus overturned the altars of the philosophies, systems of operation, and values of the world at which the worldlings assiduously worshiped.

He was called Jesus by the Angel Gabriel when He came from the Throne of God to announce the wondrous tidings to Mary. *"And, behold, thou shalt conceive in thy womb, and bring forth a Son, and shalt call His name Jesus" (Luke 1:31). "Thou shalt call His name Jesus," Gabriel said, ". . . for He shall save His people from their sins" (Matthew 1:21)*. Jesus, Savior, Redeemer, Deliverer, and King arose amongst His people and purchased for them the victory.

The Trumpet

From the first day of His showing in Israel, Jesus trumpeted forth the divine call to all men to follow Him into the battle of righteousness against the forces of evil. That trumpet call has reverberated throughout the centuries from that day until now. From sea to sea and from pole to pole – there is no place where its voice has not been heard. As it was in Gideon's day, today also there are few who have the courage and faith to arise and follow Him into war. But the echoes of that trumpet still sound forth the clarion call to go forth into battle against all the armies of sin, disease, and satanic influences.

The uplifted voice of Jesus' trumpet also reached to the Throne of His Father in Heaven in its call for help in this titanic fray. Mighty angels were dispatched to help and empower Him to victory. *"And there appeared an angel unto Him from heaven, strengthening Him" (Luke 22:43)*. Also His Almighty Father joined Him in the peak of the battle for Paul wrote, *". . . to wit, that God was in Christ, reconciling the world unto Himself, . . ." (2 Corinthians 5:19)*.

Before Heaven and Earth He openly declared His purpose to redeem and deliver His people from His enemies.

Loudly, He declared with the voice of a trumpet His challenge to them. "The thief came to steal, kill and destroy, but I am come to give My suffering oppressed sheep abundant life," He trumpeted, openly challenging His enemies, both seen and unseen.

The Pitcher

Jesus, the fulfillment of the deliverer that Gideon typified, fought the ultimate battle of deliverance for the world and set the captives free. He triumphed over the enemy hosts of darkness at Calvary. His weapons were an earthen pitcher, a torch, and a trumpet.

His earthly body was the clay pitcher in which was hidden the living flames of infinite love. Flames fueled by the oil of the Holy Spirit were poured out upon Him without measure. He carried within Himself the light of the world well concealed inside the earthen body of a village carpenter – a body especially made by the Master Potter to contain that living light, ever shining yet never seen, until the appointed time of revelation.

That clay pitcher would carry the flaming torch until the day of attack. However, the glorious light of Redemption and the cleansing fire of love that were hidden within the earthen pitcher of the Redeemer could not yet shine forth into the outer darkness of this lightless, forlorn world. First, there had to be that earth-shaking, shattering blow by the wood of the Cross to the earthen Vessel of Jesus. Only then could the fire and light of redeeming victory shine forth into the stygian atmosphere of this lost world.

At the precise moment appointed from eternity, that Pitcher was rent with a thunderous sound that echoed throughout the corridors of eternity. At the sound of that rending shattering blow, all hell was terrified with a lethal fright; His enemies fell as one in abject, total defeat, never to have the power to raise their kingdom again. The blow that broke that Earthen Pitcher caused the earth to shake and the sun to hide its face. To His enemies it was the explosive thunder of doomsday that brought routing pandemonium to all the forces of darkness.

That divine God-fire He carried within His human body was carefully nurtured and never allowed to diminish throughout His life on earth. The glorious saving light of God remained successfully hidden from all enemy eyes throughout the life of Christ. Only once was that radiant fire-light allowed to shine forth, and then for just a brief moment. His friends on Mount Tabor were allowed a brief glimpse ere they fell unconscious under the mystery-light of it.

On that day on the Mount of Transfiguration, He permitted the light to shine forth to James, John, and Peter in that transcendental hour. It was like a ray from the lighthouse of Divinity shining into the blinding darkness of the tempestuous sea of captive earth. It shone forth from that glory-mount as a ray of light flashing through history, as a beacon that calls the lost mariner home.

And The Light Shined

At the precise moment, preappointed from the foundation of the world, He being lifted up to the vantage point of His Cross, sounded forth the demolishing voice of His silver clarion's omnipotent declaration, *"It is finished!"* With the force of a thousand exploding stars, His words crashed into the ears of the spirits and unseen forces of infernal darkness. His words brought them into dreadful confusion and routed them forever into eternal devastation from which they could never recover.

Simultaneously, with the powerful challenge of His trumpet, there crashed into the void of eternal darkness and ruin, the horrendous sound of the shattering of the Clay Pitcher. With overpowering and insupportable energy, the released flames of vengeful light shattered the deluding, self-sufficiency that reigned in the encampment of outer darkness. How that mortifying sound, echoing and reechoing in relentless fury, pounded into the ears of the pride-drugged, warring spirits! In the same instant they suffered the immortal pangs of defeat by that catastrophic light blinding their eyes before they could begin to man their defenses.

Christ's implacable enemies felt the pain of the united voice of the trumpet and the resounding crash of the shattering Pitcher. Their sound entirely surrounded the enemy camp and crashed into the ramparts of Sheol like ceaseless peals of cosmic thunder. It struck ever increasing and remorseless terror into their unrepentant hearts. They were thrown into such self-demolishing panic and self-immolating fury that their ravaging power was inverted upon their own necks in devastating force. It was Gideon's victorious battle reenacted and magnified by an immeasurable factor.

The Man Alone

Immoveable, the man, Jesus, waited and defiantly declared, in the power of the Holy Spirit, His triumph in the face of His hideous foes. With the shining light of divine love and the trumpet sounding forth eternal Redemption, He stood steadfast and unwavering against all the onslaughts of the hosts of darkness.

Suddenly, with the speed of celestial light and with a universe-shaking cry of triumph, He sprang from the Cross into the midst of His enemies. With the might and power of His irresistible light, He sped into the chaotic darkness of the enemy's own encampment. Countless rays of divine light, sharp calamitous swords of light, slashed through vulnerable spirits of outer darkness. The shields of darkness that protected the spirits of evil were pierced by that light as if they were no more than gossamer illusion. With relentless force He cast them down into eternal ruin and defeat, forcing the king of hell to surrender his throne and give Him the keys of death and hell.

Another Trumpet Call

The note of faith in His Father that He blew on His silver trumpet that day resounded also in mighty reverberations that echoed throughout the corridors of time of the whole human world. The voice of His trumpet called His people to arise and join Him in the cause of *justification-by-faith* and Redemption's grace. With such mighty power He sounded His clarion that His call eclipsed even Michael's trumpet on Sinai that called a nation unto holiness.

"Save Thyself. Save Thy clay vessel," shouted the human emissaries of hell — the soldiers, the priests, the thieves, and gawking people – to Jesus on the Cross. But the Divine Gideon won the great battle for deliverance for all His captive people at the Cross – by giving Himself, by laying down His life. Divine love surrendered to the clay-shattering blows of the Cross. Jesus was crucified and broken in the sight of all men – becoming a public spectacle, even as the pitchers of Gideon's men were broken before the enemy's camp.

He knew – as man could never know – that within Him was the cleansing fire and the irresistible power of redeeming light of the Almighty Jehovah Shalom. On the Cross the pitcher of His earthen body had to be broken to release the fire-and-light-power of God into the terrified faces of the impenitent, deceitful princes of wickedness that abode in eternal darkness. Only thus could the enemy be overcome and the oppressed go free. His carefully concealed torch – blazing, alight forever – could only be released through the shattered clay of His broken body.

The Dawning Light Arises

From the black cave of His tomb, that gloriously flaming torch arose in mighty resurrection light of hope. From the black hole of death there arose into this forlorn and desolate world a light from the flame of hope that burns forever, eternally fueled by the anointing oil of the Holy Spirit that continually flows from the high Throne of the Almighty. That light and fire, alive with the flame of His love and holiness, set aflame the torch carried in every clay pitcher of His three hundred.

Jesus' arrogant adversary recognized the dreaded sound that day. It was a sound that still echoed in his ears from the days of earthly Gideon. Centuries before, into the outer darkness of the infernal regions, the sound of three hundred clay pitchers smitten and shattered thundered forth foretelling their doom. The devastating light and consuming fire released into the terrified eyes of the arrogant foe brought forth a fearful anticipation of a more deplorable day to come.

That day of reckoning came when on the Cross the terrible, hell-quaking sound of the Divine Pitcher, smitten and broken, resounded in hell. And at the same instant, the divine trumpet ordered the unseen hosts of light into battle. As a sound of searing light, hell heard the note of final damnation resounding throughout the infernal regions, and that omnipotent sound entered fatally into the heart of the prince of darkness.

The self-deified prince of darkness, denuded of all his vaunted power, had the truth of his vulnerability and mortality revealed. He fell as Baal of old in helpless defeat in the midst of all his hosts. He had no defense against those irresistible secret weapons of trumpet, pitcher, and torch. His time of oppressing God's people ended forever. He was utterly defeated by the divine God-man, Gideon. For He . . . *"Forasmuch then as the children are partakers of flesh and blood, He also Himself likewise took part of the same; that through death He might destroy him that had the power of death, that is, the devil" (Hebrews 2:14).*

"I am the Resurrection and the Life," Jesus-Gideon declared to His oppressed people, "and because I live, you too shall live." He had triumphantly overcome, and by the power of His own faith and love, He won the battle and delivered His people. He crushed the oppressor – destroyed his tyranny and purchased freedom for all. He could stand and declare to His oppressed people:

"Come unto Me, all ye that labour and are heavy laden, and I will give you rest. Take My yoke upon you, and learn of Me; for I am meek and lowly in heart: and ye shall find rest unto your souls." "I am the Resurrection, and the Life: He that believeth in Me, though he were dead, yet shall he live" (Matthew 11:28-29 and John 11:25).

Today the good tidings are spread with glad voices from city to city, hamlet to hamlet, cave to cave, hiding place to hiding place – "Jesus has overcome; the enemy is defeated. We are free; Christ has set us free!"

It is no wonder that the oppressed people of God arise out of their dens of darkness and gloomy fears to gather in ever increasing streams into the great gathering of His Church. Singing and glorifying their Jehovah Shalom, the

Prince of Peace, they come from the east and west, from the north and south. They praise God for such a mighty deliverance wrought by redeeming love.

The bystander need not wonder, when he draws nigh to the house where they gather, that he hears music, dancing, and great rejoicing. If such a one would care to listen, he would discover the good news that he also is invited to feast his famished heart at the table of deliverance that Jesus, the Divine Gideon – even Jehovah Shalom – has spread.

"Ho, every one that thirsteth, come ye to the waters, and he that hath no money: come ye, buy, and eat; yea, come, buy wine and milk without money and without price" (Isaiah 55:1).

"And the Spirit and the bride say, 'Come.' And let him that heareth say, 'Come.' And let him that is athirst come. And whosoever will, let him take the water of life freely" (Revelation 22:17).

Books by Dr. R. Edward Miller

Romance of Redemption
Written by an unknown author, this ancient romantic history of Ruth is not only a historical incident, but it is also an allegory – drawn by the Holy Spirit from the life of a young Moabitess – which depicts the progress of a soul from its sinful depravity to bridal union with her Husband-Redeemer. Ruth's correct choices and responses to the happenings in her life – combined with her faith, love, and obedience – accurately reflect the factors in a believer's life which develop that fruitful bridal relationship with Christ.

Secrets of the Kingdom
Contains eleven allegories (three of these, previously published in **The Prince and the Three Beggars**, have now been expanded and enhanced) which share some of the secrets of God's ways and workings in His Kingdom. Through these allegories, the reader can see behind the veil and discover some of the Secrets of God's Kingdom.

Victory in Adversity
> Tells of outstanding incidents in the lives of God's servants, illustrating how victory was snatched from the jaws of defeat. A source of deep encouragement during times of trial or trouble.

Thy God Reigneth
> Tells of the beginning of the outflow of God's river of revival in Argentina and its flowing from 1949 to 1954.

Story of the Argentine Revival
> Combines **Thy God Reigneth** and **The Flaming Flame** (now out of print) into one volume. **The Flaming Flame** tells the story of continued revival in Argentina. Once again, Missionary/Pastor Miller ascends Prayer Mountain where God gives him instructions to pioneer new churches, build Bible homes for training young people, and form children's homes for orphaned children. It tells of the struggles of faith, prayer, and obedience as he and his wife, Eleanor, build that work day by day "according to the pattern given on the mount."

Books of Annie's Visions
> Record the visions received by Annie and retold by Dr. R. Edward Miller. By revealing some of the hidden workings of God in the invisibles beyond the limits of time and sense, these books help the believer to enlarge his concepts of God and make the Heavenly City more real:
>
> > **I Looked and I Saw the Lord (Look I)**
> > **I Looked and I Saw Mysteries (Look II)**